# THE EPISTLES OF JOHN

# THE EPISTLES
# OF JOHN

## by
## HERSCHEL H. HOBBS

THOMAS NELSON PUBLISHERS
Nashville · Camden · New York

Published in Nashville, Tennessee, by Thomas Nelson, Inc. and distributed in
Canada by Lawson Falle, Ltd., Cambridge, Ontario.

Printed in the United States of America.

Unless otherwise noted Scripture quotations are from the King James Version of
the Bible.

**Library of Congress Cataloging in Publication Data**

Hobbs, Herschel H.
    The Epistles of John.

    Bibliography: p. 172.
    1. Bible.   N. T. Epistles of John—Commentaries.
I.   Title.
BS2805.3.H6     1983          227'.9407          82-22524
ISBN 0-8407-5274-1

Dedicated to the Memory of
ERNEST DAVIS
who was preaching when I publicly professed my faith
in Jesus Christ as God's Son and my Savior,
and who baptized me.

# Contents

# Introduction

Anyone familiar with the Gospel of John finds himself at home in the Johannine Epistles. In them there is not only the same simplicity of language and style, but also the similar depth of meaning as that found in the Fourth Gospel. This is especially true of 1 John.

Second and Third John are the shortest books in the New Testament. Curtis Vaughan notes that each contains less than 250 Greek words, and "could easily be written on a single sheet of papyrus (see 2 John 12)" (p. 12). * Because 2 John contains much that is found in 1 John, someone has called it a "cut-down" version of the first epistle.

First John may be called more accurately a tract or homily (McDowell, p. 188). It does not follow the usual form of a letter, having no salutation in which the author identifies himself, no address, and no farewell. Second and Third John are personal letters, the former addressed either to a church or a lady, (see 2 John 1), and the latter to a person and through him to a church.

---

*See bibliography for cited references unless otherwise described.

## I. Authorship

The same person obviously wrote both 2 and 3 John, in which the author calls himself "the elder" *(ho presbuteros)*. Both describe the addressees as those "whom I love in truth" (RSV). Note the similar use of "paper and ink" (2 John 12) and "ink and pen" (3 John 13), as well as the hopeful expectation of seeing them soon in person and talking to them "face to face" or "mouth to mouth" *(stoma pros stoma)*.

Internal evidence also suggests one author for the Johannine letters (compare 1 John 4:1-3 and 2 John 7; 1 John 2:7-8 and 2 John 5-6). Furthermore, McDowell (p. 189) lists similarities between the Fourth Gospel and 1 and 2 John which suggest a common authorship for all three of them. A. H. McNeile (p. 305) points out differences in these writings, but concludes that "the verdict reached after careful linguistic analysis by R. H. Charles and A. E. Brooke that the Fourth Gospel and all three Johannine epistles were penned by the same person has not been overthrown."

McDowell (pp. 189-191) gives a rather thorough analysis of the external evidence of the early church fathers to the effect that these writings are from the apostle John. He notes that they are closer to the events by 1800 years than twentieth-century scholars. Therefore, "it seems reasonable, in the absence of positive evidence to the contrary, to accept the testimony of the early church fathers." The illusive "elder" or "Presbyter John," whom some claim as the author of the Fourth Gospel, need not be identified with the "elder" in 2 and 3 John. It is reasonable that the aged John would refer to himself as such. Papias, whom

Eusebius quotes in his *Ecclesiastical History* (3,39), referred to the apostles and elders.

The writings of the Essenes among the Dead Sea Scrolls have shown that the thought patterns of John ("light" and "darkness") are those of Palestine in the latter half of the first century. We may conclude that John the apostle wrote the Fourth Gospel and the epistles.

## II. Date and Destination

The date of the Johannine epistles hinges on the date of the Gospel of John. Not many years ago many scholars saw John as thoroughly Greek in background. They dated it in the second century, one as late as A.D. 165, but the trend in recent years has been to affirm a date in the last quarter of the first century. We may safely assume that the Gospel and epistles were written prior to Revelation which must be dated about A.D. 95, one year before the death of Domitian.

Archaeology has played a major role in this turn of events. We have noted the effect of the Dead Sea Scrolls. The discovery of the pool of Bethesda, exactly where the Fourth Gospel places it, shows that the author had a knowledge of Jerusalem prior to its destruction in A.D. 70—not a later *tourist's* knowledge as some have insisted—and therefore supports the authorship of John the apostle.

The oldest fragment of the New Testament which has been found is a piece of papyrus upon which is written John 18:31-33,37-38. Reliable papyrologists (students of papyrus manuscripts) date it not later than the first half of the second century. It is now in the John Rylands Library of the University of Manchester, Manchester, England.

When time is allowed for copies of the Gospel to be circulated and copied, this probably places the original writing in the last quarter of the first century.

Other examples could be cited. But as McDowell (p. 191) says, "In a remarkable way recent papyri and archaeological discoveries have tended to confirm the tradition that the Gospel and epistles of John have come down to us from the last quarter of the first century." It has been speculated that 1 John was written as a synopsis of the Gospel, and was released at the same time. However, it is more likely that each book was written separately and in the order in which they stand in the New Testament.

No one can say with certainty as to the destination of the epistles. Second and Third John each contain an addressee, but no place is mentioned in either letter. Evidently John was intimately related to the readers of 1 John (see "My little children," 2:1; "Beloved," 2:7; 4:1,7,11; "little children," 2:12,28; and "children," 2:18). In all likelihood 1 John was written to the churches mentioned in Revelation 1:11 and chapters 2 and 3, and possibly other churches. The other two epistles could have been written to persons in any one of these.

## III. Purpose

The principal purpose in writing 1 John was to refute the false teachings of the Gnostics and to comfort and encourage those in danger of being deluded by their teachings. This also was the underlying purpose of the Gospel of John. But as McNeile points out, in the Gospel the emphasis is upon Christ's eternal relationship to the Father while that of 1 John is His relationship to men.

Second John was written to assure "the elect lady" that her children remained true to the faith; Third John emphasized hospitality and condemned Diotrephes for his overlording attitude and practice.

Since the main concern in the Johannine epistles is Gnosticism, a few words should be said about this philosophy. It was somewhat of a hodge-podge containing elements of Greek philosophy, Judaism, and the Mystery Religions. It taught salvation through knowledge (*gnōsis*) rather than through faith. This *gnōsis* involved secret knowledge known only to its initiates; the higher in this system one rose the more *gnōsis* he received.

Basic in their concept was the dual idea of God as absolutely good and matter as absolutely evil. How could a good God create evil matter of the universe? To solve this dilemma they *imagined* a series of beings called *aeons* coming out of God in a descending order, each having less deity than the one above it. The lowest being in this chain possessed enough deity to enable it to create, but only enough to create evil matter. When the Gnostics came into contact with the Christian faith, they identified Christ as this lowest aeon. Thus they regarded Him as less than God, a created being, almost a demon since He was said to have created evil matter. Robert Law (p. 31) says that the Gnostics threatened to undermine the gospel message by "deifying the devil," while at the same time dethroning Christ.

With regard to Jesus Christ they divided into two groups. The Docetic Gnostics (from *dokeō*, I seem) said that Christ did not have a real flesh and blood body, but only seemed to have one. Thus they denied the humanity of Christ. The Cerinthian Gnostics (named for their leader Cerinthus, a contemporary of John in Ephesus) held that Christ neither was born nor did He die. To them Jesus was born naturally to Joseph and Mary. The *aeon* Christ came upon Him at His baptism and left Him on the cross. They denied the deity of Jesus.

The Gnostics were further divided in conduct: ascetics and libertarians or antinomians. Some, holding to the evil of matter, withdrew from society, but others, separating *spirit* from *matter,* said that what the body did had no effect on the spirit. This led them into all kinds of immorality. The Nicolaitans (Rev. 2:6) are said to have been of this group. Clement of Alexandria (*Strom,* ii, 20) said that they were as "dissolute as he-goats," a testimony which is also supported by Tertullian and Hippolytus.

First-century Gnosticism has been called "incipient Gnosticism" which reached its full development in the second century. However, it may have reached a greater development in the latter half of the first century than once was thought. It was a vicious system which cut squarely across Christian truth. Warnings against it are reflected in John's writings, Colossians, Ephesians, and the Pastoral Epistles.

# 1 John

# ONE

# The Reality Of
# The Gospel

*1 John 1:1-4*

---

Outline

---

We live in an age which bows before the shrine of Science. Nothing is exempted from its cold analysis, including the Bible and its teachings. Since Jesus Christ is the central figure in the Bible's message, His person and work have been the focal points of biblical analysis. He has been placed under the microscope of doubt and submitted to the scalpel of human reason.

However, this is no new phenomenon. Beginning in the first century and continuing to the present the principles of ancient Gnosticism have been one of the major battlegrounds in this struggle. For this reason a study of 1 and 2 John holds great value for us—the neo-Gnostics are still with us.

The outcome of this struggle affects the nature and

reliability of the gospel itself. John addresses himself to the heart of the matter in the opening verses of 1 John. It is because of eyewitness accounts of John and others who companied with Jesus that He stands more authenticated today than ever before.

At best Gnosticism was a vague, vaporous system of thought. Paul called it a philosophy characterized by empty deceit (Col. 2:8). In its mysticism it promised much, but delivered little. Like the rivers of Damascus which flow merrily through the city only to disappear in the dry, thirsty sands of the desert, so Gnosticism appealed to sophisticated intellects but left them a barren waste.

This was true of pagan philosophy generally. It was constantly spinning noble thoughts and pointing to lofty heights of living. But it was unable to empower men to scale those heights. It was a matter of do-it-yourself as one sought to pick up himself by his own boot straps. One ancient philosopher is reported as saying something like this: "I do not know how God will save man. It may be by some god or god-man." This is probably as near to divine revelation as pagan philosophy ever came.

By contrast, the early Christian preachers declared the simple realities of the gospel. Rather than to enter into needless debate with those whose minds were closed to truth in favor of vain speculation, they proclaimed what God in Christ had done to save man from his sinful state. For example, underlying the Corinthian problem about the bodily resurrection (see 1 Cor. 15) lay the philosophy of Plato. He taught that *spirit* is everything and *matter* is nothing. Therefore, according to him, at death the spirit lived on but the body returned to dust. To counter this teaching, Paul set forth the basic facts of the gospel: "For I delivered unto you first of all that which also I received, how that Christ died for our sins according to the scriptures; . . . was buried, . . . rose again . . . was seen" (1 Cor. 15:3-5).

John followed a similar pattern in his first epistle as he dealt with the deceitful philosophy of Gnosticism. He did not meet the Gnostics in open debate, but instead, he laid down a barrage of gospel truths before sending in his ground troops. Like Paul and John we should not be fearful of letting truth do battle with error. Error may win some skirmishes, but it never wins a war. Thus truth does not need to be defended but to be proclaimed. This John did as he began his epistle by declaring succinctly the reality of the gospel.

## I. The Heart of the Gospel (1:1-3)

As we read the opening verses of 1 John we are made aware of the close relationship that they bear to the Gospel of John. Indeed, verse 1 may well form a synopsis of John 1:1-14. Common to both are such words and ideas as "beginning," "Word," "life," the Word as life, and the beholding of the Word. These similarities are not accidental, but are used deliberately as an answer to the Gnostic heresy. McDowell (p. 195) comments, "The incarnation for John in both the Gospel and this epistle is the foundation of authentic Christianity." This is the reality of the gospel as proposed in eternity and wrought out in the arena of history. It is more than philosophical speculation; it is holy history. Human reason did not discover this history, but divine revelation made it known. For this reason we will do well to examine every word and phrase in verses 1-4.

## 1. The eternal Christ (1:1a)

"That which was from the beginning." "That which" refers to the Logos or Word in 1b. These words declare the eternal nature of Christ. "Was," as in John 1:1, is the imperfect tense of the verb *(eimi)* used to express essential being. It expresses continuous action in the past, and in this context it connotes eternal, essential being. Because He always has existed, this denies the Gnostic idea that He is a created being.

"From the beginning" further emphasizes the eternal nature of Christ. John 1:1 reads, "In the beginning." These uses of "beginning" also remind us of the Hebrew phrase "In the beginning" of Genesis 1:1. Both the Hebrew and Greek words mean "head;" from the head or beginning of the universe Christ always was. David Smith says, "The Logos already was when time began."

Thus we see the sense of "from the beginning" in 1 John 1:1. This obviously is related to "in the beginning" of John 1:1. In turn, this corresponds to the same phrase in Genesis 1:1, which throws our minds back into eternity.

The New Testament presents Christ as the intermediate agent in the creative act (John 1:3; Col. 1:15-17; Heb. 1:2). To this the Gnostics would agree, while identifying Christ as the lowest being in a chain of created beings emanating from God. But John parts company with them in his use of "was." "Always was" denies their idea of His having been created by insisting that Christ was co-existent with God in eternity. John 1:1 presents Him as co-existent, and co-equal with God, even God Himself. The

Greek wording of John 1:1c means, "And the Word always was God himself."

In Colossians 1:15 Paul says that Christ is the exact manifestation ("image") of the invisible God, and the "firstborn of every creature." However, since this would make Him a created being, this is exactly what he would not have said. "Firstborn" may mean this (Luke 2:7), but according to the *Theological Dictionary of the New Testament*, the Greek word *prōtotokos* may also refer to prior being in the sense of *Lord* (vol. VI, pp. 878-79). This is obviously the sense in Colossians 1:15. Since He always was before the creative act, Christ is "Lord of every single part of creation." This is because of His essential, eternal being "from the beginning." It is a declaration of His deity.

2. The humanity of Christ (1:1b)

However, deity is only one side of the nature of Jesus Christ. Equally we must see Him as *humanity*. This refers to the incarnation of Christ as Jesus of Nazareth. It is just as great a heresy to deny His humanity as to deny His deity. Doctor George W. Truett was fond of saying, "He was God as though he were not man. And he was man as though he were not God. He was the God-Man. And never did a hyphen mean so much." Doctor Robert G. Lee also spoke of His dual nature thus: "As in eternity he leaned upon the bosom of his Father without a mother, so in time he leaned upon the bosom of his mother without a father."

Previously we noted that in his Gospel John's primary emphasis was upon the deity of Jesus, but in 1 John it is upon the humanity of Christ. Both are present in both writings; it is simply a matter of emphasis. First John 1:1a declares Jesus' deity; verse 1b sets forth Christ's humanity. In this one verse John answers both the Cerinthian and Docetic Gnostics.

Note the repeated assertion of Christ's humanity in verse 1b. John appeals to three of the five senses: hearing, sight, and touch. Also note the fourfold use of "that which" *(ho)*.

"We have heard" renders the perfect tense of completeness *(akouō)*. "We have seen" likewise is a perfect tense of the verb "to see with the natural eyes" *(horaō)*. To intensify this meaning John adds "with our eyes." The perfect tenses mean that they (the apostles) had heard and seen Jesus Christ, and these experiences remained vivid in their memory across the years. At the time of writing apparently only John was still living. But he remembered, as doubtless the others did as long as they lived.

Then John suddenly changed verb tenses from the perfect to the aorist tense. The latter denotes point action or a single act. "We have looked upon" renders *theaomai* (note "theater"). It denotes an intent, contemplative gaze (Vaughan, p. 21). William Barclay says that it means "to gaze at someone, or something, until a long look has grasped something of the meaning and significance of that person or thing" (compare John 1:14, "beheld").

"Our hands have handled." It is a verb used of touch. Jesus used this verb in Luke 24:39 as a challenge to His disciples to prove by touch that He was not simply a spirit, but possessed a real body.

At this point we can understand why John changed verb tenses. Whereas the perfect tenses express an extended seeing and hearing, the aorist tenses denote one special event. While some question this, it seems quite obvious that the aorist tenses refer to the one experience on resurrection Sunday night when the disciples not only looked with contemplation upon the risen Christ, but they also touched Him to see that His resurrection body was real (see Luke 24:39; John 20:27). Thus they were convinced that they were looking upon Him who had died but was alive again. Smith, stressing the point action of these verbs, says that it was "a spectacle which broke upon our astonished vision." The disciples were convinced as to the true nature of their risen Lord.

John identifies the one of whom he is speaking as "the Word of life." "Life" renders *zōē* which in the New Testament refers to spiritual or salvation life (see John 1:4; 3:16). He is not only the living Word, but He imparts His life to all who believe in Him as Savior (see John 1:12). This designation as "the Word" also involves the deity of Jesus Christ (see John 1:1,14); He was/is God incarnate. "That which was from the beginning" and "the Word of life" may be considered as parenthetical marks enclosing all in between. So that John says that the one who possessed full humanity also possessed full deity. He was no imaginary aeon of the Gnostics almost bereft of deity, but God Himself in human form.

### 3. The manifested life (1:2-3a)

Verse 2 is a parenthetical statement which shows how the facts stated in verse 1 were possible. In the Incarnation God revealed Himself as redeeming love. He completely identified Himself with man, apart from sin, so that man might see this revelation in terms of his own understanding. Therefore, Jesus could say, "He that hath seen me hath seen the Father" (John 14:9). What we see Jesus doing, we see God doing.

The key word in verse 2 is "manifested." Note that it

appears twice. Used often in the New Testament it occurs most often of God or Christ, or of man in his relation to them. Note its use in John's writings of Christ's incarnation (John 1:31; 1 John 3:5,8), of His appearance after the resurrection (John 21:1,14), and of His second coming (1 John 2:28). Basically the word means to bring to light or to make known what already exists. He who always was the divine Logos or Christ became tangible and visible in Jesus of Nazareth. Both uses of *manifested* in verse 2 are aorist passive forms, which denotes the historical fact that "the life was manifested" as an act of God. This eternal Life which was "with the Father" eternally was at a given point in time made manifest to the apostles and to other believers. "With the Father" reads, literally, "face to face with the Father," expressing equality of being. In John 1:1 it reads, *Pros ton theon;* here in verse 2 it reads, *"Pros ton patera."* The idea is the same, and refers to the pre-existent state of Christ. It refutes the Gnostic claim that Christ was an inferior created being.

In a sense "was manifested" corresponds to "the Word was made [became] flesh" (John 1:14a). However, the latter phrase merely expresses the *historical event;* the former in this context implies a continuing experience. It more exactly parallels "we beheld his glory" (John 1:14b). It covers the whole of Jesus' ministry, not just one phase of it. This is emphasized by "we have seen" (1 John 1:2b). Here again we have the perfect tense as in verse 1, "to see with the natural eye." They had seen Jesus Christ with their very eyes, and that seeing continues in memory.

Once again John strikes a powerful blow at both the Docetic and Cerinthian Gnostics. Christ did have a real flesh and blood body, and He was present in Jesus of Nazareth throughout the Incarnation.

In this one verse we have it all: (1) divine revelation ("was manifested"); (2) human verification ("have seen"); (3) witness to the fact ("bear witness"); (4) and the gospel message ("shew unto you").

Verse 3a summarizes the matter. For emphasis John repeats that what they have seen and heard they now declare as a public proclamation. Robertson (p. 206) calls this repetition "a thoroughly Johannine trait." What the apostles and other early Christians had experienced first-hand formed the whole of their gospel message. Through our experience of faith in Christ we know that their witness is true; so in our turn we must make it known to others. Thus, Christianity has spread down the ages—and will continue until He comes again.

4. The purpose of the gospel (1:3b)

The goal of the gospel is to produce the wonderful relationship which the word "fellowship" *(koinōnia)* describes. Today we speak of church *membership;* the New Testament speaks of Christian fellowship. The Greek word means "having all things in common" or "sharing," which is more than friendship or even the blessed relationship which Christians enjoy together. It involves the sharing of both privilege and responsibility in our relation in Christ. As such we are "heirs of God, and joint-heirs with Christ" of all that God is and has (Rom. 8:17). Note that Paul adds: "If so be that we suffer with him [responsibility], that we may also be glorified together [privilege]." He hastens to say that the *glory* will outweigh the *suffering* so that the latter is not to be compared with the former (see 8:18).

"Fellowship with us" (1 John 1:3) does not mean that John and his readers did not already have this. But this prelude reminds them that this fellowship is first with God the Father and God the Son. Indeed, Christian fellowship is impossible apart from the saving experience with God in Christ.

This also serves to introduce his discussion of this theme in 1 John 1:5 to 2:6. John is concerned that this fellowship will not be disturbed by Gnostic teachers who, on the one hand, denied the humanity of Christ, and, on the other, denied the deity of Jesus. John challenges his readers to be true to the basic doctrine upon which their faith rests. The teachings of the Gnostics were more than semantics; they struck at the heart of the Christian faith.

We cannot repeat too often that the Gnostics are still with us. Anyone today who denies the deity of Jesus and/ or the humanity of Christ is a neo-Gnostic. He is not an advanced thinker, but merely parrots the heresy of these ancient teachers. Furthermore, we have only to look at the disturbance in Christian ranks today to understand John's emphasis upon the need for a solidarity in Christian fellowship. His words are not merely ancient teachings applicable only to his day, but rather, they are timeless truths which speak to every generation of Christians. This is especially true today when every facet of our faith is subjected to critical scrutiny.

## II. The Purpose of the Epistle (1:4)

"And these things write we unto you, that your joy may be full."

The Greek manuscripts vary between "your" (*humōn*) and "our" (*hēmōn*). The true reading is difficult to determine. If we follow the former (KJV), the sense is that the readers' joy may be full. If the latter (RSV), it means that

John's joy may be full as he recounts the story of the Incarnation and also sees his readers standing firm in the faith. Both ideas make sense.

"May be full" renders what is called a periphrastic perfect passive form (the main verb used with "to be"). The perfect tense is the tense of completeness (see "complete," RSV). It may read "may be made permanently full." This verse echoes the words of Jesus in John 15:11: "These things have I spoken unto you, that my joy might remain in you, and that your joy might be full." John was present when Jesus spoke them; and now years later he repeats their substance for the benefit of those who know Jesus only by faith in Him.

Thus John closes his marvelous introduction. He also sets the stage for further teaching as the Holy Spirit through him leads Christians of all ages to a further knowledge of the truth.

# TWO

## The Blessed Fellowship

*1 John 1:5–2:6*

---

### Outline

---

A friend once told me that he and his wife were making a trip of three days alone by car. In jest he asked, "What will two people who have been married for thirty-five years find to talk about all that time?" I am certain that they found plenty about which to talk.

This led me to think of my fifty-four-year marriage (1927-1981) to Mrs. Hobbs. We were first *strangers*, then *acquaintances*, then *sweethearts*, then *husband and wife*. Our years have produced a *fellowship* which has grown deeper and sweeter. At the human level this is an example of the divine fellowship which Christians have with God and with each other. John writes about this latter fellowship in 1 John 1:5 to 2:6.

The *fellowship* which the apostle introduced in verse 3, is now discussed at length. It is a fellowship which is rooted in God and which expresses itself in our relation to our fellow-believers. Indeed, it is a fellowship "with the Father, and with his Son Jesus Christ" (1:3b) which overflows into the relationship of Christians with one another.

## I. The Fellowship With God and Man (1:5-7)

Because the nature of Christian fellowship is the result of our relation to God, John places the greater emphasis upon the latter. Without it Christian fellowship is impossible. As Ramsay (p. 249) says, "If we lose sight of the ethical nature of God, we miss the truth on which all Christianity is based and land in moral confusion. The purity of the Christian corresponds to the purity of God. Without this moral kinship there is no fellowship."

### 1. The divine origin of fellowship (1:5)

In introducing this discussion of fellowship, John makes a profound statement concerning the nature of God. Since all Christian fellowship originates in Him, those who experience it must correspond to His nature.

"This then is the message which we have heard of [*apo*, from] him, and declare unto you, that God is light, and in him is no darkness at all" (v. 5). In verse 5*a* "him" refers to Christ the subject of John's words thus far. The preposition rendered "of" refers to the source of the message, which could mean that Christ is either the intermediate or the ultimate source. Since the "message" concerns God, John evidently refers to Christ as the intermediate source in His full revelation of the Father. Jesus said, "My doctrine [teaching] is not mine, but his that sent me" (John 7:16). And in John 1:18 the apostle says, "No man hath seen God at any time; the only begotten Son, which is in the bosom of the Father, he hath declared [exegeted] him."

And what is the message? "That God is light, and in him is no darkness at all." "Light" is symbolic of *good*; "darkness" depicts *evil*. This contrast is found often in the Old Testament (see Job 30:26; Ps. 107:14). It is also a recurring theme in John's Gospel (see 1:5; 3:19-21; 8:12; 11:9-10; 12:35-36,46). The writings of the Essenes, found among the Dead Sea Scrolls, use this contrast repeatedly. McDowell (p. 197) notes that the closest affinity of the New Testament, especially John, with these Scrolls is this contrast of light and darkness. Incidentally, this affinity supports a first century date for the Johannine letters, showing that this contrast was current in first century Jewish thought. It also shows the Hebraic rather than the Greek background of John's writings.

Furthermore, in John 1:4-5,7-9, Christ is called "Light." It speaks of the oneness of Father and Son, attesting the full-deity of Jesus Christ. Here again John strikes a blow against the Gnostics.

"Light" refers to the holy, righteous nature of God, which also involves His inapproachable glory. Some interpreters see "light" as referring to God's revelation of Himself, the complete revelation being through Christ.

However, in contrast to "darkness," the idea refers primarily to God's holiness.

Typically, John emphasizes this truth by expressing it both positively and negatively (see John 1:3). God is the very essence of light, with no darkness at all in Him. Hebrews 1:3 calls Christ the "brightness [outshining] of his glory;" in Him the fellowship of God and man is made possible. Since God is light, the fellowship must be in the realm of light. Men can have fellowship with Him only if they partake of God's holiness.

We see in 1 John 1:5 also an answer to the Gnostic heresy. They held that God was absolutely good; but they also held that the aeon Christ possessed enough evil to create evil matter. Therefore, Christ came from an evil source, that is, an evil God. John counters this by saying that in God there is no darkness or evil "at all." God's revelation is full, complete, and non-contradictory. However cleverly heretics may reason, their system falls in upon itself through contradiction.

2. The hindrance to fellowship (1:6)

Since fellowship with God is possible only as our nature and conduct correspond to His, sin hinders or makes impossible such a correspondence. "If we say" (vv. 6,8,10) introduces three false assumptions.

The first of these is to claim fellowship with God while we "walk in darkness" (v. 6). "Say" renders an aorist subjunctive form, which means "If at any time we may begin to say," or as Robertson (p. 207) says, we "up and say." The present subjunctive form for "walk" means the possibility to keep on walking in darkness, and supposes a manner of life.

One group of Gnostics, holding that spirit is separate

from matter, said that what their bodies did had no effect on the spirit, which led to libertarianism. They lived sinful lives, while at the same time claimed sinless perfection. This is contrary to the entire teaching of the Bible. Never does the Bible claim that we will achieve sinless perfection while living in our fleshly bodies.

To the contrary, the Bible teaches that the Christian's life becomes a battleground between his fleshly body with its evil desires and his regenerated spiritual self with its desire to serve the Lord. Some interpreters see Romans 7:7-24 as relating to Paul's preconversion experience, but I agree with those who see him dealing with both his preconversion and postconversion experiences. The former is found in Romans 7:7-13; the latter is seen in Romans 7:14-25. Paul is talking about his own experience, but, as T. W. Manson says, it is also the biography of every man. When the devil loses a person through the regeneration experience, he endeavors to destroy the joy and effectiveness of that Christian life.

The apostle of love occasionally can be a son of thunder. Answering a false claim John says, "We lie, and do not the truth." Robertson (p. 207) says "we lie" is "plain Greek and plain English like that of the devil in John 8:44." This reminds us of the man who had no concept of life after death. On a tombstone he saw the inscription "Not dead, just sleeping.", to which he remarked, "He ain't fooling no one but himself." So the one claiming fellowship with God, while habitually living in sin, is fooling no one but himself. Most of all, he is not fooling God.

*To do* the truth is more than *believing* or *speaking* it. Here the sense definitely is that of conduct. There can be no genuine believing of truth until it becomes a part of a person's manner of life. Brooke (p. 14) says, "To 'do the truth' is to give expression to the highest of which he is capable in every sphere of his being. It relates to action, and conduct and feeling, as well as to word and thought." To believe the truth without living it makes one doubly responsible for his failure. To speak the truth without doing it is mockery of the worst sort. This verse sets the stage for what follows in verses 7-10.

3. The walk of fellowship (1:7)

In this verse "but" is adversative as it sets its statement over against that of verse 6. The present subjunctive of "walk" supposes a manner of life "in the light." Since "God is light" (v. 5), to walk in light is to walk in keeping with His nature and will. In the Greek text primary emphasis is upon the first "in the light" (God) and secondary emphasis is upon the second "in the light" (we). Literally, the reading is, "But if in the light we keep on walking, as he is in the light" (v. 7a). Since God's nature is not compatible with darkness, only when we walk in the light can we walk with Him.

If we do the above, "we have fellowship one with another" (v. 7b). Does this refer to fellowship with God or with other Christians? Both kinds of fellowship are mentioned in verse 3. Some see the former (Calvin and Spurgeon are examples). Ronald Knox in *The New Testament*, translated from the *Vulgate* as follows: "God dwells in light; if we too live and move in light, there is fellowship between us" (see Vaughan, p. 32).

However, others (McDowell, Robertson, Vaughan) see this as fellowship among believers, which seems to be John's idea. But in the final sense fellowship with God is necessary for fellowship among Christians. We first walk

with God, and then with one another. No Christian lives
in isolation from his brethren. And fellowship with God is
shown by our fellowship with one another (Brooke,
p. 15). "We know that we have passed from death unto
life, because we love the brethren" (1 John 3:14).

This walk of fellowship is made possible because "the
blood of Jesus Christ his Son cleanses [keeps on cleansing,
present tense] us from all sin" (v. 7c). "All" without the
definite article means every single one of the whole of our
sin. Christ's blood both redeems us from the sin principle
and from committed sins (see v. 9).

Here again we see John's answer to the Gnostics. "The
blood of Jesus Christ his Son" means that Christ did have
a real flesh and blood body. *Jesus Christ* gave His life on
the cross; Christ did not leave the body of Jesus before His
death. As God's Son He is not some created being re-
motely removed from God. He is instead the eternal God
revealed in flesh for man's redemption. "I and my Father
are one," said Jesus (John 10:30). We are saved through
faith in Him, not by Gnostic *gnōsis*.

## II. The Fellowship and Forgiveness (1:8-10)

These verses teach that there can be no fellowship with
God or with each other, unless we recognize that we are
sinners, and we confess our sins. This faith results in
forgiveness and cleansing.

### 1. The delusion of sin (1:8)

Note in verse 8 the second "if we say" which introduces
another false assertion. That false assertion, literally, is

"that sin we keep on not having." "Not" renders the negative *ouk,* which is a strong denial of any guilt whatsoever. "Sin" here refers to *the principle of sin* or an evil nature. It is a denial of personal guilt or of an evil nature. The *New English Bible* reads, "If we claim to be sinless."

That some Gnostics made such a claim grew out of their concept that matter was evil, and that there was no relationship between the body and the soul or spirit. What the body did had no effect upon the spirit. Robertson (p. 208) calls this "a thin delusion with which so-called Christian Scientists delude themselves today."

"We deceive ourselves" means "we lead ourselves astray." "Deceive" renders the verb *planaō,* "to lead astray." Note the origin of our word "planet," which the ancients thought was an erratic wandering body. In typical negative fashion John adds that "the truth is not in us."

## 2. The denial of sin (1:10)

For practical purposes we will treat verse 10 before verse 9. Here we have the third "if we say," expressing a false assumption of not having committed sin.

"Have sinned" is a perfect tense preceded by the strong negative as in verse 8. It expresses action in the past which is still going on at the time of speaking, with the assumption that it will continue in the future. The perfect tense is the tense of completeness. It reads, "If we say that we have not sinned in the past, do not sin now, and will not sin in the future." Whereas in verse 8 the reference is to the *principle* of sin, in verse 10 it involves *acts* of sin. Sins are the expressions (v. 10) of the sin principle (v. 8).

Such a claim makes God a "liar." This is the word used of the devil by Jesus in John 8:44. God says, "For all have sinned, and come short of the glory of God" (Rom. 3:23). For a person to claim perpetual sinless perfection is to say that God lied. Even to claim that a former lost sinner has achieved such perfection is to deny the teachings of the Bible. Therefore, "his word is not in us." "Word" here refers to the *teaching* of God's written word. Such a boastful claim stems from a crusted conscience and from ignorance of God's word.

As Vaughan (p. 34) says, "Mark the significance of 'in us' [vv. 8,10]. Truth may be all around us, near us, and acknowledged, but when we claim sinlessness we show that it has not penetrated our souls."

This reminds me of someone who claimed that he had reached a state of sinless perfection. Said he, "I am as good as Jesus Christ, and am getting better every day." Such a statement itself approaches the sin of blasphemy. When asked if this man would get to heaven, someone said, "Yes, if he doesn't overshoot it."

Of course, if this man were reminded of some wrongdoing on his part, he probably would retreat into the old Gnostic teaching, "Oh, but that was my body, not my spirit, that did that!" So this is not Bible truth, but Gnostic heresy. If I lived next door to such a person and had a hen house full of hens, I would put two locks on the hen house door. I would be afraid that some night while his sinless soul was sleeping, his body would steal my hens.

3. The confession of sin (1:9)

It should be remembered that this verse was written to Christian people (note "my little children," 2:1), and applies to both the *principle* and the *acts* of sin.

The form of "confess" is a present subjunctive; "forgive"

and "cleanse" are aorist subjunctives. "Confess" may read "keep on confessing," but the present tense at times may be rendered "from time to time." This seems to be the case here.

So, literally, "If from time to time [when we sin] we confess our sins, he is faithful [trustworthy] and just [righteous] in order that [*hina*] he may [at the time of confessing] forgive to us the sins, and may cleanse us away from every single bit of unrighteousness" (v. 9).

"Confess" translates a Greek verb (*homologeō*), which means "to say the same thing." God says, "You have sinned." The confessor says, "I have sinned." Confession is man's part; forgiving and cleansing are God's part. Until man has done his part, God cannot do His part. However, once the sinner has fulfilled the condition, he may rest assured that God will keep His promise. He is faithful to His word and just in His dealings. "Forgive" means that God takes away our guilt; "Cleanse" means that He removes the pollution of sin.

Of course, this does not mean that man has not sinned, but that in Christ God chooses to regard him as if he has not. Paul's word for this is the "righteousness" of God which is in Christ Jesus (Rom. 1:17). "Righteousness" (*dikaiosunē*) belongs to a family of words ending in *eta* which means, not that a thing is necessarily true, but that one chooses to regard it as true. This is the sense of "righteousness" when used of God's dealings with men in Christ.

"I have sinned" are the most difficult words for one to speak. However, there is a difference between *saying* this and *confessing* it. You can *say* it as a matter of fact (Matt. 27:4), but to *confess* it calls for a broken and contrite heart

(Ps. 51:1-4). Nevertheless, confess it we must, if we are to know forgiveness and cleansing. Sin mars our fellowship with God; forgiveness and cleansing make this fellowship possible.

## III. The Fellowship and Christ's Advocacy (2:1-2)

John continues to deal with the matter of sin as it relates to fellowship with God. His purpose is to show the basis upon which God can forgive sin.

### 1. The blessed promise (2:1)

Though John thus far has referred to his readers indirectly, here he addresses them directly as "my little children." He does this as an aged teacher addressing his pupils. The address is a tender one as he uses the word *teknia,* a diminutive form of *teknon* (child). The personal pronoun adds to this tenderness: "little children of mine." Seven times in the epistle John addresses them in this manner (2:1,12–13,18,28; 3:18; 4:4), though in 2:13,18 he uses the word *paidia,* the diminutive of *pais,* boy. But the sense is the same.

"These things" may refer to chapter 1, but more likely it refers to the entire letter. Brooke (p. 23) holds to the entire epistle, but notes that "to some extent the main teaching of the Epistle has already been declared in outline" in chapter 1. Vaughan (p. 36) sees reference to chapter 1 as more in harmony with the tenor of the passage. However, John's repeated statement of his purpose in writing (2:12-14) seems to favor the entire epistle.

The purpose of the epistle is "that ye sin not," or "may not sin" (v. 2a). The aorist tense of the verb refers to an occasional sin, not to the habit of sinning. Robertson (p. 209) calls this an ingressive aorist, "that they may not begin to commit sin." The ideal is that they should not commit even one sin.

However, knowing that the probability is that they will commit an occasional sin, he adds, "And if any man sin." Here again he uses the aorist tense, occasional not habitual sin. He is not trying to condone sin, but to prevent it, while at the same time knowing the human weakness even of Christians. His statement in 1:9 might be construed by some as an encouragement toward sin. If someone *confesses* his sin with a view to sinning some more, such an attitude is not true confession. At the same time John proposes to explain how it is that God in Christ can/does forgive and cleanse the true confessor. This he introduces with the conditional phrase in 2:1b.

"We have an advocate with the Father, Jesus Christ the righteous" (note "just" in 1:9). "We have" is a present tense, "we keep on having," which is a present reality. "Advocate" is the same word used by Jesus for "Comforter" (John 14–16). The word (*paraklētos*) appears in the New Testament only here and in John 14:16,26; 15:26; 16:7. A kindred word (*paraklēsis*) is used twenty-nine times as "consolation," "exhortation," "comfort," and "intreaty." These senses may be seen in *paraklētos* as portions of the work of the Holy Spirit. Note that Jesus' use of the word refers to the Holy Spirit, while John's use refers to Jesus Christ. The two uses complement each other. Vaughan (p. 37) says, "Here on earth we have the Holy Spirit as our Advocate; in heaven we have Christ as our Advocate." With respect to the use in John 14–16, *paraklētos* has been transliterated into English as *Paraclete*. Since His work with Christians involves comfort, encouragement, and exhortation, a comprehensive term would be *Divine Helper*. In this sense the Holy Spirit is God's Advocate with us, and Jesus Christ is our Advocate with God.

Of course, "advocate" carries a legal meaning. This is a Latin derivative composed of *ad*, "to," and *voco*, "call," or "one called to." It is the Latin equivalent of *paraklētos*, *para*, "alongside," and *klētos*, "being called," or one being called alongside. In legal life it referred to a lawyer, especially one for the defense, who stood alongside a client in court. *The New Berkeley Version* reflects this as it renders the word in 1 John 2:1 as "counsel for our defense."

Therefore, Jesus Christ is our counsel for the defense "with the Father." It is our loving Father, not a stern judge limited by law, before whom our counsel pleads our case. Furthermore, "with the Father" renders *pros ton patera*, a phrase which denotes equality (John 1:1). The author of Hebrews says that Jesus Christ "ever liveth to make intercession for [*huper*, on behalf of] them" (7:25). This intercession and advocacy do not mean that God is praying to God. He also does not plead our innocence. Instead, His redemption work is always before the Father on behalf of all believers in Jesus Christ as Savior.

2. The basis of forgiveness (2:2)

Not only is Jesus Christ our Advocate before God, but He is also "the propitiation for our sins." Yes, for the whole world. This is not universalism, that is, that all will be saved, but that all may be saved through faith in Jesus. The effectiveness of Jesus' advocacy rests in His work of propitiation. The word for "propitiation" (*hilasmos*) is found in the New Testament only here and in 1 John 4:10; the verb form is used in Luke 18:13 and Hebrews 2:17. Both the noun and verb forms are used in the Greek translation of the Old Testament to denote a *covering* and *to cover* respectively.

Many interpreters object to the rendering "propitiation" in 2:2. In pagan Greek religion this word carried the idea of sacrifices appeasing the wrath of their gods. In the Bible God is seen as angry with sin, but loving toward the sinner. Man needs to be reconciled to God, but not God to man, else an offer of redemption would not be necessary. Thus the *Revised Standard Version* renders it "expiation," or a removal of that which offends God; Williams translates it "atoning sacrifice." McDowell (p. 199) is helpful at this point: "In Christ's death the cause of the sinner's enmity toward God is removed and his approach to God made possible through his union with Christ, who is the holy and righteous Advocate."

Rather than to see "propitiation" as an appeasing of God's wrath, which is an idea foreign to the New Testament, we may see it as the grounds upon which a holy, righteous, and loving God may forgive sin. God Himself provided such grounds in His Son Jesus Christ. In His atoning sacrifice He took our place when He died for our sins, and the Father authenticated His work through His resurrection. Christ's death satisfied the demands of God's holiness, and at the same time provided grounds upon which He might offer His loving grace and mercy to all who believe in His Son. Therefore, the marred fellowship between God and man is restored.

## IV. The Fellowship and Obedience (2:3-6)

This does not mean that a person can "get saved," and then do as he pleases. In Romans 6 Paul says that in our pre-Christian state we gave our powers to serve the devil, so in Christ we should dedicate them to serve the Lord.

## 1. The demand of grace (2:3)

That we are saved by God's grace is an evident fact (see Eph. 2:8-10), but so often we do not read all of this cited passage. Saved by grace through faith? Yes, but we should put equal stress upon Paul's words "created in Christ Jesus unto good works, which God hath before ordained that we should walk in them." Grace is a gift, but the miracle of grace makes demands—that we should show in our conduct what God has wrought in our hearts.

It is in this light that we may comprehend John's words. "And hereby [in this] we do know that we know him, if we keep his commandments" (2:3). The second "know" is a perfect tense. By experience we know that we have come to know and do know Him, but how do we know this? "If we keep his commandments." To know God is to have fellowship with Him. There can be no fellowship with God apart from obedience to His will and way.

People often ask, "How can I know that I am saved?" Vaughan (p. 40) answers this by commenting upon verse 3: "(1) we can know God; (2) we can know that we know Him; (3) this assurance comes through obedience to His commands." This obedience is not a rote, mechanical thing, but rather it is an inner and loving submission to God which expresses itself in outward obedience. Joy is found in doing the will of God.

The verb "keep" was used of a sentry walking his post. It means to keep watch over or to be on guard so as to obey and fulfill God's will in one's life. The present tense means that this should be the habit of one's life.

2. The pseudo-Christian and the true Christian (2:4-5)

Following his customary pattern John states, first negatively, and then, positively, how to determine if one is a false pretender or a true believer. He plays on the idea set forth in verse 3.

Negatively, one who claims to know God, yet does not keep His commandments, is "a liar, and the truth is not in him" (v. 4). "Know" is a perfect tense of completeness. John has in mind the heretics or Gnostics who claimed that obedience to God's commandments is irrelevant to a full knowledge of God. Of course, this knowledge is synonymous with fellowship with Him. The truth involved is revealed truth as seen in Jesus, and "keepeth" is a present tense expressing habitual action. To borrow a phrase that a friend of mine used years ago of one whose false life belied his professed faith, "He hasn't even waved at the Lord!"

Positively, whoever "keepeth [present tense] his word" in him, God's love "is perfected" (v. 5). This is a perfect tense of the verb meaning to bring a thing to a desired end or goal. To what does "the love of God" refer? Is it God's love for man, or man's love for God, or a God-kind of love (see Vaughan, p. 41)? Perhaps all three are involved. In this context, if one must choose, then the second seems likely. Such is proof that we are in God or in fellowship with Him.

3. The example of Jesus (2:6)

In Jesus we have the perfect example of fellowship with God the Father. He was in the Father, and the Father was in Him. The will of Father and Son was one. His total purpose of being was to do His Father's will and to finish His work.

If we claim to have the habit of abiding in God, we "ought" to order our lives in keeping with Jesus' life. "Ought" expresses a moral obligation (see 1 John 3:16; 4:11; 3 John 8). To do this we must have with the Father a constant relationship of love, obedience, trust, service— whatever we see Jesus doing, we also must do. We will not do these things perfectly as Jesus did, but we must be on our way. By the help of the Holy Spirit, we always pursue the goal.

# THREE

## The Abiding Commandment Of Love

*1 John 2:7-17*

---

### Outline

I. The Old–New Commandment (2:7-8)
1. The old commandment (2:7)
2. The new commandment (2:8a)
3. The age of light (2:8b)
II. The Revealing Light of Love (2:9-11)
1. The darkness of hate (2:9)
2. The light of love (2:10)
3. The blindness of hate (2:11)
III. The Warning Against Misdirected Love (2:12-17)
1. The basis of the warning (2:12-14)
2. The warning given (2:15a)
3. The warning explained (2:15b-17)

---

One of the most beautiful poems on love was written by Elizabeth Barrett Browning to her husband Robert Browning (*Sonnets from the Portuguese,* XLIII).

How do I love thee? Let me count the ways.
I love thee to the depth and breadth and height
My soul can reach, when feeling out of sight

45

For ends of Being and ideal Grace,
I love thee to the level of everyday's
Most quiet need, by sun and candlelight.
I love thee freely, as men strive for Right;
I love thee purely, as they turn from Praise.
I love thee with the passion put to use
In my old griefs, and with my childhood's faith.
I love thee with a love I seemed to lose
With my lost saints,—I love thee with the breath,
Smiles, tears, of all my life!—and, if God choose,
I shall but love thee better after death.

In finite degree this describes the love we should have for God, because He first loved us to the uttermost. Of this divine love John writes in 1 John 2:7-17.

John has been called "The Apostle of Love." Those holding to his authorship of the Fourth Gospel see him as identifying himself as the disciple whom Jesus loved (John 20:2; 21:7,20). A tradition says that as an old man in Ephesus, John gathered his disciples about him and said, "Little children, love one another."

His emphasis upon such love is seen in this commandment, which is found six times in 1 John (Vaughan, p. 43; see also 2 John 5). Vaughan quotes Findlay in calling it "*the* commandment" of the epistle. When one considers the many exhortations to love one another, one can see that love is the prevailing theme of the letter.

There are probably three reasons why John places so great an emphasis upon this love. (1) Jesus commanded it. (2) Gnosticism may have been disturbing the fellowship in the churches. (3) It may have been John's way of opposing the proud, contemptuous, and loveless attitude of the Gnostics.

46

## I. The Old—New Commandment (2:7-8)

In verses 3-5 John has spoken of the importance of keeping God's commandments. Now in a rather peculiar fashion he singles out one particular commandment and applies it to his reader's present relationship. While not stating it openly, it becomes evident that he is thinking of the commandment to love. He has cited Jesus' manner of life which they are to reproduce in their own lives (v. 6).

### 1. The old commandment (2:7)

In the best texts John addresses his readers as "beloved" (*agapētoi*), which is his favorite term of address found in his epistles (3:2,21;4:1,7,11; 3 John 1-2,5,11). David Smith (p. 175) says, "About to enjoin love, he begins by loving."

The commandment which John writes is not "new." This renders *kainos*, not new in time (*neos*) but new in kind or quality. Rather he writes an "old" commandment, which means ancient as opposed to new in time. This old commandment his readers "had from the beginning," a phrase not found in the best texts of 7b, but is genuine in 7a.

"Had" renders an imperfect tense. They had this commandment in the past and continued to have it. "Heard" is an aorist tense, denoting a time when they first heard the commandment. But when had they heard it? Assuming that the old commandment has to do with love, it could be that they had learned it from the Old Testament. Indeed, the Jews summed up the Ten Commandments by combining verses from their scriptures (see Deut. 6:4-5; Lev. 19:18b; Matt. 22:37,39). The sense is to love God absolutely and one's neighbor as himself. Certainly this fits the word "old."

Brooke (p. 35) notes the possibility, even probability, that this "old" teaching must be included. But he recognizes the difficulty of pinpointing the time. He also rightly notes that verses 7-8 must be interpreted in context. In this case that context would be the so-called *newer (neos)* teachings of the Gnostics "which placed knowledge higher than love." John is saying that long before the Gnostic heresy his readers had been taught the primacy of love.

2. The new commandment (2:8a)

In this verse a casual reading might see a contradiction between verse 8 and verse 7. But a closer examination reveals otherwise. The key is found in "again" *(palin)* which may read "in another sense," or "at the same time." John may be saying, "In one sense it is not a new commandment, but in another sense [or at the same time] it is a new commandment." Robertson (p. 211) cites John 16:28 as another usage of "again." This commandment is not *new* in time but in kind or quality *(kainē)*. Here the reference definitely is to Jesus' words in John 13:34. "A new commandment I give unto you, That ye love one another; as I have loved you, that ye also love one another." This corresponds to "which thing is true in him and in you" (v. 8a). Jesus loved His disciples absolutely, and they are to love one another to the same degree.

Jesus' commandment was new in that He was a living expression of love. Because the Jews heard it so much, the summary of the Decalogue had become mere written words. This is seen in the Jewish lawyer's question, "And who is my neighbour?" (Luke 10:29). To him the command to love his neighbor as himself had become a subject to be debated, not a principle to be practiced. Therefore, Jesus' command to love one another was new in kind. As embodied in Jesus, man had never seen such love. In Him it became not merely a nice phrase but a startling reality. He showed that it was the only realistic way for people to live. Sadly, the world has yet to learn or admit this.

Love was new to John's readers because it opened an entirely new way of life. "As a new thing it came to them, and was manifest through them to the world. It brought a new day in the relation of man to man . . . The world looked on and said, 'Behold how these Christians love one another'" (Conner, p. 64). This brings us back to the question as to when John's readers had heard this "from the beginning." This probably dated from the time they became Christians and began to receive instructions as to how they should live. John reminds them that this new commandment is still binding upon them, regardless of what the Gnostics might be saying.

3. The age of light (2:8b)
"Because the darkness is past, and the true light now shineth."

The verb tenses are present. *The Twentieth Century New Testament* (TCNT) reads, "For the darkness is passing away and the true Light is already shining." Although "darkness" is symbolic of evil, here it may also imply the pre-Christian era prior to God's full self-revelation in Jesus Christ. Literally, John 1:9 reads, "He was the true Light which shines on every man, coming into the world." We are also reminded of John 1:5, which reads literally, "The Light in the darkness keeps on shining, and the darkness was not able to overtake [overcome] it."

So John speaks of a process. The age of darkness has not been completely removed, but the age of Light has dawned, and for that reason the darkness is in process of passing away. This will not be fully accomplished until the Lord comes again. But the final outcome is assured.

"True" used of light means the true or genuine light as opposed to the false or spurious. Vaughan (p. 47) notes that this is a favorite word of John. Used only five times in the New Testament other than in John's writings, he uses it twenty-three times—four times in 1 John. Here it denotes the true Light in Christ as opposed to the false speculations of the Gnostics.

Previously we noted that the neo-Gnostics are still with us. Their teachings of darkness still try to extinguish the Light. But the Light keeps on shining in the darkness. Darkness and light cannot exist in the same place, because whenever the Light of Christ shines into a life, darkness must flee.

## II. The Revealing Light of Love (2:9-11)

Outward attitudes reveal inner conditions in our lives, and love for others or love's opposite, hate, reveals whether we live in light or darkness. To put it another way, whether or not one is a Christian.

### 1. The darkness of hate (2:9)

The darkness is in process of passing away, while the true light is already shining, driving out the darkness. But darkness still remains, and so long as this is true the perfect day has not dawned. John deals with darkness which still exists even among some professed believers, which is in direct contrast to true believers. Therefore, he treats them as "the ones hating" and "the ones loving."

The one who says that he is in the light, but who hates his brother, is still in darkness. To claim to be in the light is to claim to be a Christian. "Hateth" is a present tense denoting a continuous condition, a fixed attitude. "Brother" could refer to any man, not simply a blood brother. It is a sin to hate or despise any person. Even if you do not like his ways, you should love him as a person.

However, the use of "brother" here should be seen as a fellow-Christian. The Greek word for "brother" comes from a root word which means *out of the same womb* or having the same source of life. The common source of spiritual life is God in Christ, hence the term "brother." Such a person who hates his Christian brother "is in darkness even until now." "Until now" is emphatic; it means up till this moment. One may be a part of the Christian community, but not a part of the *fellowship* because he is still abiding in darkness. Though the light continues to shine, he has not come to the light. He has always been in darkness, and still is.

Mere outward profession is not enough, but the attitude of one's heart and the outward deeds of his life must confirm such a profession. Sadly the condition John describes in churches of the first century still exists, which is evidenced by strife within churches today. John's words should cause us to examine our hearts with respect to those of the church fellowship. At times even Christians permit darkness to reign in their relationship with their brethren. We should both believe in Christ and permit him to be Lord in our lives.

2. The light of love (2:10)

Conversely, the one loving his Christian brother "keeps on abiding" (present tense) in the light. This is the key word in this verse. Christians may cease to agree, but they should never cease to love.

"There is no occasion of stumbling in him." "Occasion

of stumbling" renders *skandalon* (note "scandal"), which was used of a stumbling-block or trap. This may be understood in either of two ways. First, it may mean that nothing in the loving Christian's life causes him to stumble. Smith (p. 176) renders it "there is no occasion of stumbling, nothing to trip him up and make him fall, in his case." Other translations reflect the same idea: "There is nothing within him to cause him to stumble" (TCNT); "There is nothing to make him stumble" (NEB); "In the light there is no pitfall" (Moffatt).

Secondly, others see this as the loving person having nothing in his life to make other Christians stumble. This is the usual sense of the word. Note other translations: "Puts no hindrance in anyone's way" (Goodspeed); "He is no hindrance to others" (Williams). Robertson (p. 212) cites Westcott who contends that John may mean the latter in verse 10 and the former in verse 11.

However, it is possible to see both ideas in verse 10. If one has no occasion of stumbling within himself, he will not be a pitfall or trap into which others will fall. We are responsible for our fellow-Christians as well as for ourselves (Heb. 12:1-3,12-16). Failure to have a loving heart sets traps into which others may fall.

3. The blindness of hate (2:11)

This verse repeats the thought of verse 9, but with an additional comment. The one hating his brother not only keeps on walking in darkness, but also he "knoweth not whither he goeth, because that darkness hath blinded his eyes." "Knoweth" (*oida*) means that he really does not know where he is going. The picture is that of a blind man groping in the dark, stumbling and falling over every obstacle in his path. Someone has described utter darkness as a dark room full of black cats at midnight. Such is the state of one who hates his brother.

The life of such a person is aimless, without a goal or purpose for living. His entire being is centered in self rather than in others. Furthermore, he misses life altogether, like the mole who burrows beneath the green grass, beautiful flowers, and breath-taking landscape. It is his nature to do so because he is blind both physically and spiritually. He first is "in" darkness, and then he "walketh" in darkness.

We are told that in Echo River in Mammoth Cave in Kentucky the fish have eye sockets but no eyes. Smith (p. 176) explains this phenomenon thus: "The neglected faculty is atrophied." In bygone days mules were used in mines to pull the coal cars. I read somewhere that one day each week they were brought out of the mines in order to preserve their eye sight. Likewise, we must come out of the darkness of hate in order that we may see.

## III. The Warning Against Misdirected Love (2:12-17)

Having laid down the general principles concerning love and hate, John is preparing to warn his readers against the danger of misdirected love. The love involved is *agapē*, the highest kind of love, which involves selflessness and absolute loyalty to its object. Therefore, it must be a directed love bestowed upon the proper object.

### 1. The basis of the warning (2:12-14)

Some interpreters see these verses as foreign to the context. One calls it a "wedge" inserted between verses 11 and 15. However, I agree with the idea that John's purpose is, before giving his warning, to assure the genuine Christians that he has every confidence in them and in their firmly fixed faith.

Another difference of opinion centers in the author's change of verb tenses: "I write" (*graphō*, present tense, vv. 12-13) and "I have written" (*egrapsa*, aorist tense, v. 14). Smith (p. 177) sees the aorist tense as referring to the Fourth Gospel. Vaughan (p. 50) cites Robert Law who claimed that an interruption while John wrote caused the change of tenses at the end of verse 13. After a delay he returned to his writing. The aorist tense in verse 14 reflects his repetition of the thoughts in verses 12-13, after which he resumes his treatment. This seems less likely. There is a similarity of thought, but not exact wording altogether.

A more likely explanation is that the tenses were changed deliberately for emphasis. He uses what is called an epistolary aorist, which may be translated as a present tense (Robertson, McDowell, Brooke, Vaughan).

"Little children" seems to be an inclusive term referring to all Christians (see 2:1). "Fathers" and "young men" may be seen symbolically as referring respectively to the more mature in the faith and the less mature. John's little children have had their sins forgiven (perfect tense of completeness) by virtue of Christ's person and redeeming work (v. 12). For this reason they "have come to know and still know" (perfect tense) the Father (v. 13c).

Then John speaks to all the little children, old and young in the faith (v. 14). The "fathers" *have known* (perfect tense) Him from the beginning or longer than the young men. The latter, while not old in the faith, are strong and vigorous, and have known Christ who is from the beginning (1:1), and "have fully overcome" (perfect

54

tense) the evil one (vv. 13-14). The Word of God constantly abiding in them makes them strong and victorious. "The evil" one could be a reference to the Gnostics because they were tools of the devil.

Ramsay (p. 267) says, "The man whose mind is stored with right principles and true conviction is clad in triple steel." Furthermore, Vaughan (p. 53) comments that these young men are well-equipped for the struggle before them. "They have been given divine strength, they have the Word of God within them, and they have the confidence born of victories already won against the enemy." Paul's words in Ephesians 6:10-20 form a good commentary on this matter.

### 2. The warning given (2:15a)

Having expressed his complete confidence in his readers, John now gives his warning: "Love not the world, neither the things that are in the world." "Love" is a present imperative form preceded by the negative particle *mē*. It could mean to stop loving the world, but in this context it more likely means not to have the habit of loving the world.

"World" (*kosmos*, note our "cosmos") is a favorite word of John. Out of one hundred and eighty-seven occurrences in the New Testament, John uses it one hundred and six times (Gospel: seventy-nine times; 1 John: twenty-three times; 2 John: one time; Revelation: three times). He uses it of the beautiful natural world in which we dwell (John 1:10; 1 John 4:17; compare Pss. 8; 19); it is used of the entire sinful race which God loves (John 3:16); and it is used of a pagan social order which takes no account of God (John 14:30; 15:18-19; 16-30; 1 John 5:19). This last is the sense in verses 15-17, and may be seen as a synonym for "darkness." Love is forbidden both for the world and the *things* in it (see v. 16).

The verb for "love" in 2:15a is *agapaō*. In classical Greek it had various uses, but in the New Testament it is used for both divine and Christian love. In the negative sense, as here, it forbids the Christian bestowing upon the sinful social order and the things pertaining to it a love which belongs only to God and other persons.

While the word is not used, Jesus expressed the same idea in the Sermon on the Mount. "No man can serve two masters . . . Ye cannot serve God and mammon" (Matt. 6:24). "Serve" means to serve as a slave. Each owner demands absolute loyalty, and you cannot give it to both. Also in Matthew 6:22-23 he spoke of the eye as the light of the body. If the eye be "single" or focused on one thing (God and his will), the entire body is full of light. But if it be "evil" (diseased, bad) or has double vision, the body is full of darkness. Commenting on verse 24 Robertson (*Word Pictures*, I, p. 57) calls such a person "cross-eyed or cock-eyed . . . We keep our [sic, one] eye on the hoarded treasures of earth and roll the other proudly [or piously] up to heaven." Divided effort and interest explains the unhappiness in the lives of so many Christians.

3. The warning explained (2:15b-17)

If we *love* the *world*, the *love* of the *Father* is not in us (v. 15b). In both cases the word for "love" is the same (*agapē*). If this highest love is bestowed upon the world, then this love cannot be given to God. Augustine used the figure of a bridegroom making a beautiful ring for his bride. If she, in turn, loves the ring more than the bridegroom, she loves the *thing* more than she loves its maker.

There are many lessons to be learned from Genesis 1.

But running throughout it is the thought that we should not worship created things but their Creator. Love for the world rather than for God actually is idolatry, which Paul defines as *covetousness*, the desire for more—whether it be money, sex, or worldly glory (Col. 3:5).

"For all that is in the world . . . is not of the Father, but is of the world" (v. 16). These he lists as "the lust of the flesh, and the lust of the eyes, and the pride of life." In both cases "lust" renders the word for "desire." It may be good or evil, depending upon how we use it. In Luke 22:15 Jesus used both the noun and verb in the good sense. In our text it is used in the evil sense. W. Hersey Davis once defined sin as an illegitimate expression of a legitimate desire. God gave us certain desires, but Satan endeavors to cause us to express them in an evil way, and that *desire* becomes *lust* (Matt. 5:28).

"Pride of life" is most revealing. "Life" renders *bios*, not *zōē*, which is John's usual word for "life." He uses *zōē* sixty-four times out of one hundred and thirty-four times it appears in the New Testament—thirteen times in 1 John. It denotes the inner or spiritual life. But here he uses *bios*, the outer or animal principle of life (note "biology"). He employs it only one other time (1 John 3:17) where it is rendered "good", or that which sustains biological life. Here it may mean worldly position and possessions. *Bios* is the kind of life which man shares with all other creatures. One living only at this level is living as an animal, not as a child of God.

"Pride" renders a word which means a boaster, one who indulges in braggadocio or empty talk. It denotes one who foolishly trusts in his own resources and ignores the power of God and the rights of others. It is an apt description of the rich fool (Luke 12:16-21).

John's list of worldly things reminds us of Genesis 3:6. Eve saw that the tree was good for food (physical appetite), pleasant to the eyes (aesthetic nature), and desired to make one wise (ambition). These are the three areas in which Satan tempts us. He used the same temptations on Jesus (Matt. 4): bread (physical appetite, lust of the flesh), jump from the pinnacle of the temple, do the risque (lust of the eyes, aesthetic nature), glory of world dominion (ambition, pride of life). He failed with Jesus, but he succeeded with Eve and succeeds with us. Satan has no new temptations. Why should he when he catches us with these age-old ones?

There is nothing wrong with physical appetite, love of the beautiful, and ambition; they are of the Father. But when Satan perverts them in us they are "of the world," and flood the world with tears, just as in Eden.

John closes this theme by showing their transient nature (v. 17). "The world passeth [is passing away], and the lust thereof." Because life is so fleeting, it will soon be gone, if we center our love in the fleshly and material. We will be left with nothing. If I live only to satisfy the lusts of the flesh or eye, then I live only for passing *pleasures.* If I boast about my possessions, not knowing that they really possess me, I can lose them in a day. At death I certainly must leave them behind. Having lived only for these things, the *bottom line* of my account with God reads *Zero*, for I am held responsible for how I *lost* my immortal soul (see Matt. 16:26).

Whoever does the will of God "keeps on abiding for ever" or "unto the age." To paraphrase the poet, I have only one life to live. It soon will be passed. And only that which I do for God will last. God's will is that I trust in His Son as my Savior, and dedicate my life to His service.

So we end where we began. We must obey the new–old commandment—love God absolutely, and our neighbor as ourselves. Yea, to love the Lord and the brethren even as He loves us. This is both the law and the gospel.

# FOUR
# The Christians And
# The Antichrists

*1 John 2:18-29*

---

## Outline

---

One of the worst tragedies in modern times was the mass murder at Jonestown. It was the awful result of troubled people following the wrong kind of leader. But it is microscopic in comparison with the worldwide blood-bath of World War II. The source of it was the same: a troubled nation following the wrong leader. Infinitely greater in depth and scope is the multitude of lost souls who followed false spiritual leaders through the ages. This helps us to comprehend John's words in 1 John 2:18-29.

Up to this point in 1 John the author has dealt largely with general ideas. Veiled references have been made concerning those false teachers who were troubling the churches. Knowing the thought background of the epistle, we are able to understand these references.

Now that he has laid a proper background, John uses plain language in dealing with the problem. But for the interpreter questions still remain. What does he mean by "the last time"? Who are these people: "the antichrist" and the "antichrists"? Did John expect the immediate return of the Lord? What is the nature of the believers' obligations? We will seek to answer these questions as we study this passage.

## I. The Last Hour (2:18a)

Here again John addresses his readers by calling them "little children." He tells them, literally, that it is "a last hour" ("the last times," KJV). The indefinite article "a" is used because there is no definite article in the Greek text. Various interpretations have been given to this statement. One holds that the end of the age is near. This view thinks John is mistaken about the time element. The phrase "the world passeth away" or "is passing away" (v. 17) and a definite reference to the Lord's return in verse 28 suggest an imminent return.

Obviously that event was not near because almost nineteen hundred years have passed since John wrote these words. It makes him lay claim to a knowledge which even Jesus said that He did not possess (Mark 13:32; compare Acts 1:7). More than one New Testament writer hopes that this event will occur in his lifetime (see 1 Cor. 15:51; 1 Thess. 4:17). But they also show the possibility that this will not be the case (see 2 Cor. 5:1-6; Phil. 1:23). Their watchful hope was in accord with Jesus' own teachings (see Matt. 24:42-44). Some generation will be alive when He returns. We should share the New Testament writers' expectant hope.

Another position views "a last hour" as a time of crisis in John's day. Thus John speaks of the general condition of that period, not of the end of the age. Certainly the Gnostic heresy created such a crisis.

A third view is that this phrase refers to the entire Christian era—the time between Christ's first coming and His final return. In his *The New Testament: A New Translation* Olaf M. Norlie translates it, "My children, it is the final age of the world." A similar phrase "the last times" (1 Pet. 1:20) or "in this last period of time" (NEB) was so regarded.

In his sermon at Pentecost Peter interprets the coming of the Holy Spirit at Pentecost as a fulfillment of Joel 2:28-32. An examination of this passage shows that the "great and the terrible day of the Lord" (v. 31) is related to the end of the final age. But Peter's emphasis is upon an event near the beginning of the Christian era. In other words, the "last days" refers to the time in which God deals with man through Christ, or the era of grace. If we keep this in mind, we will not speculate about the end time which the Father has put in His own authority (Acts 1:7).

It seems that this is what John means by "a last hour." It leads him into a discussion of *antichrists*. The work of Christ was felt throughout the ancient world; Satan was opposing it through *antichrists*.

## II. The Antichrists (2:18b-23)

The word "antichrist" (*antichristos*) means just that—against Christ. This word appears in the New Testament only here and in 1 John 2:22; 4:3; 2 John 7. Robertson (p. 215) agrees with Westcott that "John's use of the word is determined by the Christian concept, not by the Jewish apocalypses."

### 1. The antichrists' relation to God's people (2:18b-19)

John calls them "antichrists," not *pseudo-Christs* (*pseudo-christos*). However, McDowell (p. 204) probably is correct in thinking that John means the false Christs against which Jesus warned (see Matt. 24:4-5,23-25; Mark 13:5-6,21-23). A false Christ is against Christ. The primary purpose of Jesus was to warn against self-proclaimed political-military messiahs or imposters offering to lead the Jews in a revolt against Rome. Such "messiahs" were a major contributing factor in setting off the Jewish War (A.D. 66-70) which ended in the destruction of the Jewish nation. But Jesus carefully pointed out that these false saviors, plus wars and rumors of wars, were not signs of His second coming. We should keep this in mind as we examine John's words about antichrists.

John reminds his readers that they have heard that "Antichrist comes," a present tense with a future effect. Here the singular form refers to a certain person, hence it should be capitalized. This singular form appears only here and in 1 John 2:22; 4:3; 2 John 7. Probably John refers to the one whom Paul calls "that man of sin" or "of lawlessness" (2 Thess. 2:3-10). This points to an individual who as the very epitome of evil will appear near the end of the age. He will be "the son of perdition" who opposes and exalts himself above God, who as God, "sitteth in the temple of God," but who will be slain by the breath of Christ's mouth. Through the centuries futile attempts have been made to identify this person with certain individuals who appear to be the very essence of wickedness. However, the fact that John mentions this person without any further description shows that the early Christians knew exactly what "antichrist" meant and needed no further description.

Even as John wrote there were "many antichrists," or those opposing Christ. "Are there" renders a perfect tense of the verb meaning "to become" or "to come into being" (*ginomai*). This is in contrast to the verb "was from the beginning" (1:1) by which John speaks of Christ. "Was" is the imperfect tense of *eimi*, "always was", expressing his essential, eternal being. But antichrists come into being and are still with us. For anyone who is against Christ is an antichrist.

In verse 19 the apostle is more specific in identifying these "many antichrists." "They went out from us, but they were not of us." "Out from us" is emphatic. "Out from us they went." They evidently were merely nominal Christians, but were not true believers. In Acts 20:29-30 Paul told the elders of the church in Ephesus that grievous wolves would strike the flock from without: "also of your own selves shall men arise, speaking perverse things, to draw away disciples after them." This prophecy had been fulfilled in Ephesus and elsewhere. Ronald Knox's translation reads, "They came of our company, but they never belonged to our company."

An attack from without tends to draw Christians together, but heretics within the fellowship scatter the flock. Throughout history persecution from without has purged and strengthened the churches, but divisions and broken fellowship are the results of pretenders within them. Probably, John is referring to Gnostics who had infiltrated the church fellowship. He calls them "many antichrists," a title which fits many troublemakers in churches today.

John adds that if they had been one with them in faith, they would have remained with the church. But in leaving they revealed "that they were not all of us." "Might be made manifest" is an aorist passive subjunctive. The passive voice shows that their leaving was a part of the divine plan. God removed their mask of false pretensions in order to show their true nature.

We should not see these as true Christians who were lost again. Rather, they were not Christians at all, but merely pretended to be such. One mark of true discipleship is perseverance in the faith. Failure to continue proves the falsity of one's profession. B. H. Carroll was fond of saying, "When you see a 'star' fall you can know it is not a star" (Vaughan, p. 63). In like manner, when you see a *Christian* fall, you can know that he is not a Christian.

In the Greek text "all" translates *pantes* without the definite article. So it means *every one of the whole*. The *Twentieth Century New Testament* correctly translates this, "That they do not, any of them, belong to us."

2. The true people of God (2:20-21)

In contrast to the above, John points out the true people of God. "But" is adversative, setting true over against false believers. "Ye have an unction [anointing] from the Holy One, and ye know all things" (v. 20). In both uses "ye" is emphatic, written out and also present in the verb form. This anointing (*chrisma*) is the peculiar possession of Christians.

"Anointing" comes from *chriō*, to anoint. From it also

comes *christos*, the anointed one, or Christ. The "anointing" does not refer to the act but to that with which one is anointed, such as anointing oil. It is used also as a metaphor for the Holy Spirit. Repeatedly in the New Testament we are taught that simultaneously with regeneration the Holy Spirit indwells the believer (John 14:17; Acts 10:44; 19:6; Rom. 8:9). "Holy One" refers to Christ.

To understand John's use of "anointing" we must note that when the Gnostics initiated someone into the secrets of their group, they supposedly received enlightenment and insight unknown to ordinary believers. So John *borrowed* their word to say that through Christ the Christian is anointed with the Holy Spirit. The word rendered "anointing" (unction) appears in the New Testament only here and in 1 John 2:27 where it is translated "anointing" (KJV). The Gnostic's claim to anointing is false; the Christian's anointing is true, which enables him to distinguish between the false and the true.

While the Gnostic anointing was only for a select few, the Christian anointing is for every believer. In verse 20 the best manuscripts read, not "ye know all things" but "ye all know it." "Know" renders *oida*, meaning perceptive knowledge or really to know. "All" without the definite article reads, "Ye know it, every single one of you." Every true believer really knows this experience.

John concludes this particular thought by assuring his readers that he has not written to them because they do not know the truth. To the contrary, he has written because they do know it and that no lie is a part of truth (v. 21). Literally, "Not even one lie is of the truth." For a thing to be of the truth it must be absolute truth unmixed with any error.

A lie is a lie. Truth is truth. The most vicious of all lies is one which contains a half-truth. Reasonable people can spot a whole lie with little difficulty. However, if a statement is half-lie and half-truth, one is more likely to accept the lie rather than the truth. Many lies gain entrance into one's heart by riding on the coat tail of a bit of truth. This is a favorite trick of heretics. They make a statement which will not stand up by itself. But then they quote a verse of scripture—out of context—so that to the unwary it seems to support the lie. Scripture should never be interpreted out of context.

Classic examples of proving something by quoting Scripture out of context are (1) to prove that you should hang yourself: Judas "went and hanged himself" (Matt. 27:5); "Go, and do thou likewise" (Luke 10:37); (2) to prove that Eve was the mother of a possum: a possum is living; "Eve . . . was the mother of all living" (Gen. 3:20). Although this logic is ridiculous, it is no more so than some proof-text methods of Bible interpretation.

3. The antichrists' beliefs (2:22-23)
    With reference to a lie John now returns to the antichrists. Their beliefs identify them. Note that as John proceeds he becomes more specific.
    "Who is a liar but he that denieth that Jesus is the Christ? He is antichrist, that denieth the Father and the Son" (v. 22). Unquestionably, the apostle has the Gnostics in mind. He strikes at the very heart of their beliefs which are a denial of the gospel, which explains John's strong language at this point. The Greek text reads, "Who is the liar?" The definite article shows that anyone teaching Gnostic doctrine is a liar (Vaughan, p. 64, calls such an "arch liar"). If such a person is not a liar, then no-one is one.

The liar, then, is anyone who denies that Jesus is the Christ. This charge is directed at the Cerinthian Gnostics. As noted previously, Cerinthus taught that Christ neither was born nor did he die. The *aeon* Christ came upon Jesus at His baptism and left Him on the cross. Of course, this denied the deity of Jesus. To the Cerinthians Jesus was just a man, born naturally and had all the imperfections common to all men. Therefore, they distinguished between the historical Jesus and the Christ. To them even Christ was a created being who barely possessed any deity.

Further, John continues, "He is [the] antichrist, that denieth the Father and the Son." Note that in the Greek text the definite article is used with "antichrist," which points to some definite person. This is reflected in the translations of Goodspeed: "He is the real Antichrist—the man who disowns the Father and the Son," and Weymouth: "He who disowns the Father and the Son is the antichrist." In this statement John is not thinking of the "man of lawlessness." In my judgment Weymouth is correct in not capitalizing "antichrist." Robertson (p. 217) is more likely correct in seeing this as a reference to Cerinthus himself. He was a contemporary of John and also lived in Ephesus. Evidently the apostle held him in great contempt. A tradition says that upon entering one of the public baths in Ephesus, John learned that Cerinthus also was there. John rushed out of the bath, not wanting to be under the same roof with him.

This denial of the Father and the Son involves both the God-aeon idea, and also the virgin birth of Jesus. If Jesus was born naturally, then God was not His Father and He was not God's Son in a peculiar, eternal way. It denied Jesus' deity and the whole redemptive process of God in

Christ. Therefore, it denied the very heart of the gospel.

In verse 23 John reinforces his statement in verse 22. "Whosoever denieth the Son, the same hath not the Father." The New King James Bible reads, "Whoever denies the Son does not have the Father either." Only in Jesus Christ do we have the full revelation of the Father (Matt. 11:27) and the only access to Him (John 14:6).

To deny the full humanity of Christ and full deity of Jesus is to shut off such an one from God altogether. As one has said, the God of such is the product of his imagination—an idol. Alexander Ross (p. 173) adds that "the man who denies the Son . . . is an orphan, a fatherless child in the vast loneliness of the universe."

So-called modern theologians would do well to ponder these words. McDowell (p. 205) considers John to say that the antichrists were atheists. "In later times [even recently] there have been theologians [one such was a historian posing as a theologian] who declared that God was dead, but they refused to give up Jesus. However, the Jesus they clung to was not *the Son*. Their heretical views of Christ separated them from the Jesus of the New Testament." When one departs from the clear New Testament revelation, he paints himself into a corner from which there is no logical escape.

The latter half of verse 23 (KJV) is in italics, denoting that no such words are in the Greek text. However, they are found in the best Greek texts which were unknown at the time when the King James Version was translated. "He who confesses the Son has the Father also" (RSV).

When John wrote the words in verses 22-23 he could well have had in mind Jesus' words recorded in John 5:23. The Father has committed all judgment to the Son "that all men should honour the Son, even as they honour the

Father. He that honoureth not the Son honoureth not the Father which hath sent him."

## III. The Obligation of Believers (2:24-29)

Having dealt with the heretics, John now turns his thoughts to the true believers. They are to show their faith by remaining steadfast despite the Gnostic teachings.

### 1. The exhortation to steadfastness (2:24-26)

In the Greek text verse 24 begins with an emphatic pronoun. It sets true Christians over against the Gnostic heretics. Literally, "As for you, what ye heard from the beginning, let it keep on abiding in you." This refers to the message of the gospel first preached to them before the coming of the vicious Gnostics. If they abide in this message, they will continue to abide in the Son and in the Father. "Ye" in verse 24c is also emphatic. "Ye yourselves will continue to abide in both the Son and in the Father." "Abide" means to live, as in a house. While they live in both the Son and the Father, this abiding is proof that they are truly Christian.

John reminds them of God's promise of eternal life or "life of the age" (see v. 25; John 3:16; 5:24). Eternal life is not simply the length of time after death, but the quality of life which we have now and eternally, as soon as we believe in Christ. John wants to keep them from being disturbed in their faith by the Gnostic attempts to "seduce" them or lead them astray (v. 26; see 1:8, "deceive").

### 2. The certainty of Christian faith (2:27)

Already John has reminded his readers of their "unction" or "anointing" by Christ with the Holy Spirit (v. 20). Now he mentions it again. The sense here is similar to verses 20-21. Because of this anointing the Spirit abides in them (John 14:17). Jesus said that the Spirit would guide them into all truth (John 16:13) and will glorify Jesus Christ (John 16:14). While Gnostics belittle Him, the Spirit glorifies Him. *Any system of religion or theology which glorifies the Holy Spirit above Jesus is not of the Holy Spirit,* for, Jesus said, "He shall glorify me."

The statement, "ye need not that any man teach you," is not intended to degrade teaching itself because Christianity is a teaching religion (Matt. 28:18-20). John himself was a teacher addressing his "little children" or pupils. His purpose is to show that they had no need for Gnostic teachers to lead them into the deeper things of God. Their teacher is the indwelling Holy Spirit who teaches truth (John 14:17a).

Thus as the Spirit keeps on abiding in them, they are to keep on abiding in Christ—to remain true to him and to his word. This reflects Jesus' words in John 15:4-7. Note how much John's thoughts here correspond to Jesus' words in John 14–16.

"Abide" is one of John's favorite words, being used by him more than by all other New Testament writers together—twenty-three times in 1 John. In the King James Version it is rendered as "continue," "remain," "dwell," but most often as "abide." It may be seen as the equivalent of Paul's "in Christ," which involves vital union with Christ. To use Jesus' figure of the vine and branches (John 15:1-7), it means that as the branches abide in the vine, so must we abide in Christ.

It is interesting to note John's mixture of the Holy Spirit abiding in us and our abiding in Christ. Indeed, the Holy

Spirit did not come to replace Jesus, but He is the Spirit of Christ (Rom. 8:9), or Christ in spiritual presence with us. Marcus Dods calls the Holy Spirit "Jesus' *alter ego.*" B. H. Carroll referred to Him as "the other Jesus."

### 3. The blessed assurance (2:28-29)

The reason for the necessity of our abiding in Christ is "that when he shall appear, we may have confidence, and not be ashamed before him at his coming" (v. 28). This is definitely a reference to the Lord's return. "Coming" translates *parousia,* presence, or "being alongside." In non-biblical use it referred to a ruler's visit to a city in his realm. In the New Testament, especially in Paul, it is a standard term denoting the second coming of Christ. It appears only here in John's writings.

The fact of this event is certain, but the time is not. The Lord left it that way, but many people have an insatiable desire to know the future, as if they could avoid unhappy events. They are like the Irishman who said, "Faith, and I wish I knew where I was going to die. I would never go there." If I knew my future as I know my past, it probably would drive me insane. Indeed, many have become deranged because they worried about things which never happened at all.

Except in cases of prophecy God has mercifully drawn a veil over the future. For the most part, even prophecy is not dated on a calendar. This is also true of the Lord's return. One reason why God hides the future from us is to make it necessary for us to focus upon the present. The past is behind us; the future ever flees before us. The only time we have is the present.

Therefore, the Holy Spirit through John tells us to "keep on abiding in" Christ (v. 28). Here a present imperative expresses both a command and an urgency. In verse 27 he states this abiding as a fact. Now he repeats it as an exhortation (Brooke, p. 64).

"That" (*hina*, in order that) introduces the purpose for it in verse 28. When he comes, "we may have confidence, and not be ashamed at his coming." "Confidence" translates a word which basically means "freedom of speech." It expresses the attitude of children talking to their father in contrast to a slave talking to his owner. Appropriately, it expressed the idea of intimate friends baring their hearts to each other. It later came to mean "to have confidence" or boldness. "Ashamed," on the other hand, means to shrink away from someone because of a feeling of guilt. Literally, it reads "not be ashamed away from him."

The idea is that we should so live that when Jesus returns as the Judge we will not shrink away from Him with a sense of guilt, but will welcome Him in confidence and with a good conscience. Revelation 6:15-17 depicts the former; Revelation 22:20b describes the latter.

John closes this theme in verse 29 with an explanation for the confidence of the Christians. The former "know" (*oida*) expresses perceptive or complete knowledge; the latter "know" connotes experiential knowledge. Through an experiential knowledge that Christ is righteous, we have assurance that the one who does righteousness, or lives a life corresponding to His nature and will, has been born of Him.

While Paul uses the Roman legal figure of adoption into God's family, John uses the vital figure of the New Birth. In both cases the resultant idea is that of being born again into a new family, the family of God. John's usage again reflects his remembrance of Jesus' words in John 3.

Does John in verse 29 mean that one can be saved by

doing righteous deeds? Not at all. Such is contrary to John's writings. What he is saying is that since Christ is "righteous," those born of him will do "righteousness." We prove who we are by what we do. As previously stated, grace is God's gift, but it makes its demands.

# FIVE
# The Children Of God

*1 John 3:1–24*

---

Outline

I. The Privileges of God's Children (3:1-3)
   1. The recipients of God's love (3:1a)
   2. The members of God's family (3:1b)
   3. The sharers in Christ's glory (3:2-3)
II. The Evidences of Divine Sonship (3:4-24)
   1. The participants in righteousness (3:4-10)
      (1) The relation of sin and law (3:4)
      (2) The redemptive work of Christ (3:5-8)
      (3) The effect of the Christian experience (3:9)
      (4) The summation of the matter (3:10)
   2. The expression of love (3:11-24)
      (1) The heart of the gospel (3:11)
      (2) The example of Cain (3:12-15)
      (3) The love of God (3:16-18)
      (4) The assurance of love (3:19-24)

---

One of the most blessed things about being a pastor is to rejoice with parents when a new baby is born. For that reason I have always visited the mother and her baby on the day of birth. What a joy it is to look into the face of a newborn baby with the dew of heaven still on its brow, and to think of the almost infinite possibilities bound up in that one little life.

"Father" is the most beautiful designation of God. As "Father" He has one eternal, unique "Son." But He longs for others to *become* His children through faith in His Son. God is fatherly in His nature, and He longs to be the Father of all people. But He is truly Father only to those who receive His unique Son as Savior (see John 1:12). Expectedly, in treating our relationship to God, John would include the topic of the children of God. This he does in Chapter 3.

John's use of the phrase "born of him" in 2:29 suggests the wonderful relationship which Christians enjoy as children of God (1 John 3:1 to 5:12). Some interpreters include this verse in the larger body of Scripture dealing with this matter. However, verse 29 seems to climax the theme stressed thus far in the letter and to provide a transition to the new theme concerning God's children.

Brooke (p. 79) sees John's purpose at this point as an effort "to restore the waning enthusiasm of his readers, and to recall them to their first love." God in Christ has shown His love for them. They, in turn, are to respond in love for Him. If in loving God they incur the hatred of the world, their privilege as God's children far outweighs the suffering involved (see Rom. 8:14-18).

## I. The Privileges of God's Children (3:1-3)

Though the world's glory may be glamorous and enticing, it is also shallow and fleeting. The fickleness of worldly acclaim is too well known to require further treatment. What the world gives today, it takes away tomorrow.

In high school one of my classmates was Ben Chapman, a star athlete. Following his graduation he signed a contract with the New York Yankees and played in their outfield alongside Babe Ruth. After his first season with the Yankees, I asked him what it was like being a major league ballplayer. He replied, "Oh, the salary is great. What I don't like is that to the fans you are a hero today and a bum tomorrow." Eventually he became a big league manager.

I had lost track of him until one day I saw a picture of him, his wife, and his child in the church paper of the First Baptist Church, Selma, Alabama, of which our nephew, Dr. Henry L. Lyon III, is pastor. They had joined this church by letter from another congregation.

Though his baseball days have passed, his being a child of God is forever. His privileges as a child of God are permanent. John mentions three of these which are enjoyed by all of God's children.

1. The recipients of God's love (3:1a)

Many, if not all, of John's readers had formerly been pagans, or at least they lived in a pagan environment. Pagan worshippers contemplated more the wrath of their gods than their love. Understandably, John speaks of God's love in a superlative sense. McDowell (p. 207) says that verse 1a should be punctuated with an exclamation point: "Look!"

"Behold, what manner of love the Father hath bestowed upon us" (3:1a). "Behold" (*idou*) means to see with deep understanding. "Love" (*agapē*), of course, denotes divine or the highest form of love (see Rom. 5:8). But the key word here is *potapē*, "what manner of," referring to the quality and distinctiveness of God's love.

Originally *potapē* meant "of what country," but it came

to mean "of what manner or sort" (see Matt. 8:27; Mark 13:1; Luke 1:29; 7:39). Smith (p. 182) understands the word here as carrying something of its original sense. "The love of God in Christ is foreign to this world: 'from what far realm? what unearthly love?'" In any case John's usage expresses surprise at the admirable character of God's love. It, like God's peace, defies human understanding (Phil. 4:7). Arndt and Gingrich point out that in some uses it should read "how great" or "how wonderful." In 1 John 3:1 they suggest "how glorious."

We have become so accustomed to thinking of God's love that we no longer stand in awe before it. To the contrary we take it for granted. We even think of it as something which God owes us. But as we can see, the ancients did not think so. So great was the thought of God's love that it astounded them. Even the aged John, who had been a follower of Jesus Christ from young manhood, still exclaimed such love.

He adds that the Christian permanently possesses this love, which is seen in the perfect tense of "hath bestowed." The verb means "to give." God had given it and they still had it—a state of completion. We may also see in this perfective tense the abundance or overflowing nature of the Father's love; He has given it without measure. Significantly, in light of the pagan idea of their gods, John uses "Father" rather than "God."

## 2. The members of God's family (3:1b)

The result of this abundant love is "that we should be called the sons of God." Interpreters are divided over the meaning of "that" *(hina)*. Some see God giving His love "in order that" we may be called his children. Others see this merely as a statement of fact, that we are so called.

While this is a fine point, the result is that believers are His children and recipients of His love. This phrase shows the greatness of His love, that of a Father to His children.

"Sons" should read "children" *(tekna)*. It comes from the verb "to be born," so "born ones." This same word is used in John 1:12: "But as many as received him, to them gave he power to become the sons *[tekna]* of God." "Power" means "out of being", or what proceeds from one's nature. So to believers, Christ, the eternal Son, imparts His nature, and thus we are called children of God. As Brooke (p. 81) says, "It is no empty title. It is a realized fact."

This thought does not come through in the King James Version. But the oldest and best texts, as well as all modern translations, add, "and we are" or "and such we are." It emphasizes the fact that we are God's children.

In Ephesians 2:19 Paul says that Gentile believers who were once "strangers and foreigners" are now in Christ "fellow-citizens with the saints, and of the household of God." In other words, we not only are citizens of the kingdom of God, but as His children we dwell in the palace of the King.

John anticipates a question from his readers: If we are children of God, why does not the world recognize us as such? His reply is that the world does not know us, because it did not know Jesus (see John 15:18-19). In both here and John 15, the word for *knowing* means "to know by experience." The world did not know God Incarnate (Jesus Christ) when He was on earth, and for the same reason it does not know His children. The world rejects *Christians* because it has rejected *Christ*.

3. The sharers in Christ's glory (3:2-3)
If we share in Christ's rejection by the world, we will

also share in His glory when He comes again. Having spoken of our present dignity as children of God, John now speaks of our future destiny. Note that he addresses his readers with the tender word "beloved": beloved of God and of John.

"Now are we the sons of God, and it doth not yet appear what we shall be" (v. 2a). Emphasis is upon "now" and "not yet." Christians *now* have a present standing and responsibility before God as we share in both the privileges and responsibilities of sonship. It is glorious, but there is an even greater glory to come. "Appear", in the aorist passive, means to make manifest. It means that never was "what we shall be" disclosed to us. We find slight suggestions of it in such passages as John 14:1-3; 17:24-26; Romans 8:14-18; 1 Corinthians 2:9. But these are but "peeps" through the veil. The veil itself has not yet been removed to give us a full view of the glory which awaits us.

"But we know that, when he shall appear [be made manifest], we shall be like him; for we shall see him as he is" (v. 3b). Our destiny then is to be like Jesus who is like God (2 Cor. 4:6). "Know" means perceptive knowledge to the point of conviction. "Shall see" means to see with our eyes. It reminds us of "face to face" in 1 Corinthians 13:12, in contrast to the blurred image seen in polished metal. "Now I know in part; but then shall I [fully] know even as also I am [fully] known." Note the "now" and "then" of this verse. I will know Jesus then even as He knows me now. Glory unspeakable!

Someone asked me once where heaven is. I said, "I don't know, but it is where Jesus is. And that is heaven enough for me."

"And every man that hath this hope in him purifieth

himself, even as he is pure" (v. 3). "Every man" translates
*pas* (all) without the definite article, which means every
single one having this hope in Him. "Hope" means ear-
nest expectation; "purifieth" means free from contamina-
tion. It was used of ceremonial cleanliness in the
Septuagint (Greek translation of the Old Testament), and
it was used of the purification of the high priest on the
Day of Atonement before he entered the Holy of Holies.
The New Testament sense is that of cleanliness of heart,
soul, and spirit.

Of course, this latter is a matter of God's grace. But
"himself" means our total surrender to God, that by His
grace we may separate ourselves from all that defiles.
"Purifieth" is a present tense which denotes a continuous
process. We are to be pure "even as he [Christ] is pure"
eternally. We are not to judge our lives by other peoples',
but by Christ's, who is the standard or goal toward which
we are to move. The New Testament does not promise
sinless perfection while on this earth. But we have the
goal and should ever pursue it (see Phil. 3:7-17). "Our
destiny is to be conformed to the image of God in Christ"
(see Rom. 8:29; Robertson, p. 221).

Smith (p. 183) sums it up in an anonymous verse.

> Ah! the Master is so fair,
> His smile so sweet to banished men,
> That they who meet it unaware
> Can never rest on earth again.

## II. The Evidences of Divine Sonship (3:4-24)

Repeatedly in the epistle John has related conduct to
profession. A person shows who he is by what he does.

Paul says that we are saved by grace through faith *unto* good works (Eph. 2:8-10). James says that the kind of faith that saves is the kind that produces good works (James 2). John agrees with both. And he sets forth two evidences that we are children of God: righteousness (vv. 4-10) and love (vv. 11-24).

### 1. The participants in righteousness (3:4-10)

John closed chapter 2 with a reference to doing righteousness, then in 3:1-3 he digressed to speak of the wonder of God's love in Christ, our duty to strive to be like Christ, and the necessity to be pure as He is pure. This last thought brought him back to the theme of righteousness. If we are to be Christlike we must live righteously and must love as God in Christ loves.

(1) *The relation of sin and law (3:4)*—Literally, verse 3:4 reads, "Every one having the habit of doing sin, also has the habit of doing lawlessness, and sin is lawlessness." It is evident that the translation of the King James Version is misleading. For one thing, "committeth sin" suggests the idea of one act of sin, while the present tense in Greek carries the force of habitual sinning. Under temptation in a weak moment a Christian may sin, but he does not live for the very purpose of sinning. Even one sin is terrible, but there is a difference between this and a life-style devoted to sinning. We will discover throughout this section that the meaning rides upon the Greek verb tense (see 1:6-10).

In English the verb tenses primarily denote time. In Greek tenses time is secondary; the kind of action is primary. For this reason it is misleading to read the English idea into the Greek tense. The Greek language is so rich in expression that it is difficult to translate its richness into smooth English.

Despite the fact that he was one of the leading Greek scholars of his time, A. T. Robertson repeatedly refused to make a translation of the New Testament. He reasoned that it is impossible to do so without losing something in the translation. He finally relented, but died unexpectedly before he could complete his work. I was in his class when he had the stroke which took his life an hour and a half later. An enterprising student took pictures of some of the last things he did, such as Greek words written on the blackboard. One picture was of his desk. Right in the middle of his desk lay his green eyeshade on the pages of this not-to-be-finished translation.

The other misleading translation is about *transgression of the law*. In both instances the Greek simply has "Keeps on doing lawlessness" and "Sin is lawlessness." "Transgression" suggests the act, but "lawlessness" denotes the spirit which produces the act. The American Standard Version translates verse 4: "Every one that doeth sin doeth also lawlessness; and sin is lawlessness." But even here the full strength of the tense for "doeth" does not come through.

The key words in this verse are "sin" and "lawlessness." "Sin" means to miss the mark, such as an archer missing a target. It is not how near or far the arrow is from the target, but that in both cases he misses it. There are no small and large sins with God.

There are two ways one can miss a target: through bad aim, or because of a weak bowstring which lets the arrow fall short of the target. In a spiritual sense the target is the character and will of God. To have an inadequate concept of God is to shoot with bad aim. To fall short of the target means the same as to achieve the character and obey the will of God through his own strength. Because his *bowstring* is too weak his arrow falls to the ground short of the target. This latter picture seems to fit Paul's words in Romans 3:23.

"Lawlessness" (*anomia*, no law) connotes rebellion, a purposeful defiance of God. Literally, the text can read, "The sin is the lawlessness", or it may also read, "Lawlessness is sin." Every sin is rebellion against God's will. The Commandments, which express God's will, convict all men of sin. Although we make distinctions between a liar and a murderer, God says that both men cross His will. That is why James 2:10-11 says that if you violate one of God's Commandments, you are as guilty as if you had violated all ten of them. How many laws do you have to break to be lawless? Just one. How many sins do you need to commit to be a sinner? Just one. Of course, this is compounded when one makes it the habit of his life. Such a life-style is totally incompatible with the New Birth from God.

(2) *The redemptive work of Christ (3:5-8)*—Because of man's rebellious nature and/or inability to save himself, God in Christ intervened in history to provide redemption from sin for all who will receive it. This purpose is stated in verses 5 through 8.

"Know" in verse 5 (*oida*) means perceptive knowledge, and may be rendered "ye really know" (v. 5). "Was manifested" here refers to Christ's incarnation and all that pertains to it, whereas in verse 2b it is used of His second coming. "To take away our sins" is a purpose clause introduced by *hina*, "in order that he might take away our sins." "Take away" means to take up and bear away something as though it were His own. They are "our sins" (note plural), but He bore them away as though they were His own (see John 1:29).

But John hastens to add, literally, "And sin in him is not." The singular "sin" denotes the sin principle, although it is equally true that He had no *sins*. Note the emphatic position of "sin," made more so by the strong negative particle *ouk* (see 2 Cor. 5:21). This cited verse reads, literally, "The one not knowing sin experientially he [God] made sin on our behalf, in order that we might become God's righteousness in him." Though we are not righteous, God chooses to regard us as such—we share in Christ's righteousness. As sinners saved by grace we share "in his sinlessness."

On the other hand, "Whosoever abideth in him sinneth not: whosoever sinneth hath not seen him, neither known him" (v. 6). Here again the verb tenses tell the story. Every one *abiding* in Christ "does not have the habit of sinning." Conversely, "every one having the habit of sinning has not seen him, neither known him." The verbs for *sinning* are present tenses expressing repeated action in the present time. Such a person lives for the purpose of sinning.

Both "seen" and "known" are perfect tenses—to see with the natural eyes and to know experientially. Of course, both verbs here carry the spiritual idea—to see with the eyes of faith and to know through a personal spiritual experience. In other words, whosoever makes sinning the habit of life has never (past or present) had a vital contact with Christ. In both cases "not" is the strong negative *ouk*.

Following this emphatic statement John makes a strong appeal to his "little children" (vv. 7-8). He pleads that they do not allow anyone to lead them astray. "Let de-

ceive" is a present imperative expressing a command and/
or the urgency of his appeal. Those leading astray are the
Gnostics who taught that the body had no effect on the
spirit. The emphasis is upon "doeth" ("committeth,"
v. 8a); in both verses 7 and 8 it is the present participle of
*poieō.*

The one habitually doing righteousness is righteous,
even as Christ is righteous. But the one habitually doing
sin is "of the devil, because from the beginning the devil
sins as a way of life." Here in 8b we have two opposite
principles of life. On one hand, Christ lives by the principle of righteousness, as do those who belong to Him. On
the other hand the devil lives by the principle of evil, as
do those who belong to him.

Seeing the righteous one as God, McDowell (p. 209)
says, "John with unmistakable precision identifies both by
their parentage. His thesis is 'like father, like son.'" The
righteous person strives to live righteously, for he is born of
God through Christ and by the power of the Holy Spirit.
The habitual sinner lives like the devil, for he is of his
father the devil (see John 8:44). Phillips translates it, "But
the man whose life is habitually sinful is spiritually a son of
the devil." He "belongs to the Devil" (TCNT).

In verse 5 John says that Christ was manifested to take
away our sins. Here he says that His manifestation was for
the purpose of destroying the works of the devil (v. 8b).
The works of the devil are the sins which men commit,
which Paul called "works of darkness" (Rom. 13:12; Eph.
5:11). Among the Dead Sea Scrolls was found a work of
the Essenes, called "The War of the Sons of Light and the
Sons of Darkness." Although John was probably not familiar with this document he reflects the same thought in
verse 8, which is further evidence that John's writings
reflect the thought patterns of first century Palestine.

"Destroy" renders an aorist subjunctive form of *luō*, to loose. It also meant to dissolve or to break. Various meanings are given to it in the New Testament: breaking of the Mosaic law (see John 7:23); breaking up of a ship (see Acts 27:41); the destruction of a dividing wall (see Eph. 2:14). Vaughan (p. 79) suggests the meaning here that our sins bind us like chains. Christ came that He might break these chains and loose us from them.

However, we may also see the devil's works as any evil force at work in the universe (see Eph. 6:10-13). McDowell (p. 209) points out that Christ's work is to destroy the works of the devil. Why not destroy the devil himself? Eventually this will be done, or he will be removed from any work in the world when he is cast into the lake of fire (see Rev. 20:10). But returning to McDowell's thought, to have destroyed the devil in the midst of history would have been to remove man's choice between good and evil. This would have reduced man from being a person with the right of choice to some other type of being.

This is a good logical and spiritual answer to the question often heard: "Why does not God destroy the devil?" In His wisdom and mercy God will not force Himself into a person's life. Neither does He remove the element of choice and struggle between good and evil, so necessary in the development of Christian character. If God did otherwise, He would destroy man's personhood and make him a puppet.

(3) *The effect of the Christian experience (3:9)*—For this spiritual struggle against the devil, God has wonderfully endowed His people. "Whosoever is born of God doth not commit sin" (v. 9). In English this reads as though a true believer commits no sin. But again the Greek tense of "commit" has a different shade of meaning. It is the

present tense of the verb "to do," expressing habitual action. "Born" is a perfect participle denoting the completeness of the act. Such a person does not have the habit of "doing sin." He may sin on occasion, but it is not his life style.

The reason for this is that "his [God's] seed keeps on abiding in him" (v. 9b). "Seed" in this case refers to the spiritual life-principle or divine nature. Williams renders it as "the God-given life-principle continues to live in him."

As a clincher John adds, "And he cannot sin, because he is born [perfect tense] of God" (v. 9c). Verse 8 is a favorite proof text of those who claim sinless perfection. But the Greek tenses speak otherwise. In this last statement, for instance, "sin" is a present infinitive. "He cannot have the habit of sinning, because he is born of God and remains so." McDowell (p. 210) says, "The meaning is that the child of God is simply incapable of living a sinful life [as distinguished from committing an occasional sin] because the birth (begetting) from God experienced by him is an abiding reality. His character was fixed when God begot him. This character is devoid of the capacity to live in sin."

(4) *The summation of the matter (3:10)*—John sums up his discussion which began in 3:4. In so doing he divides the human race into two groups: sons of God and sons of the devil. It is all light and darkness with "no twilight" (Westcott, p. 108). They are distinguished by two simple tests: those who do or do not righteousness and those who love or do not love. He states only the negative side, with the positive side implied. "Manifest" may read "plainly distinguished" (Vaughan, p. 81).

Both "doeth" (participle) and "loveth" are present tenses, which implies that they speak of habitual conduct and attitude. Failure to do righteousness and lack of love for one's brethren are evidences that one is a child of the devil. The positive side of these denotes a child of God. In other words, outward conduct shows inward reality.

An example of the negative side of this is seen in John 8:33-39. Although by their own standards the Pharisees were righteous and loving, by God's standard they lacked these qualities. So Jesus called them children of the devil. The lack of love and failure to live righteously point back to what God has been saying about sin. John's reference to love forms a transition to what he is about to say in that regard.

## 2. The expression of love (3:11-24)

As stated earlier love is the second proof of sonship given by John. He has spoken of the love which God has shown toward us. Now he deals with our obligation to love one another.

(1) *The heart of the gospel (3:11)*—"For this is the message that ye heard from the beginning, that we should love one another." The word for "message" is found in the New Testament only here and in 1 John 1:5. It denotes the heart and substance, not the aim, of a truth of great importance (Smith, p. 185). In 1:5 it is related to the character of God. In 3:11, "message" is related to the basic duty of a Christian. Vaughan (p. 82) notes that 1:5 is a summary of Christian theology; 3:11 is a summary of Christian ethics.

The message is what John's readers heard from the beginning of their Christian experience, namely, "that we should love one another." The gospel is based upon three *loves:* God's love for us, our love for Him, and in Him our love for others. To put it another way, God's love coming down to us in Christ, our love ascending to Him through our faith in Christ, and in Christ our love extending out to all men. As you point in these various directions, you make the sign of a cross. God's greatest expression of His love for us is seen at Calvary (see Rom. 5:8). Because God so loved us, we are commanded to love one another. By loving we will show ourselves to be children of God.

(2) *The example of Cain (3:12-15)*—Here we have the classic example of the opposite of brotherly love. The first murder mentioned in the Bible was that of Cain killing his brother Abel (Gen. 4:1-8). In murdering his brother, Cain was of "that wicked one," the devil. Jesus said that the devil was a murderer from the beginning (John 8:44). Because his works were evil and those of Abel were righteous, Cain was jealous of his brother. He let this resentment fester until it erupted into murder. It was the final outcome of his character and attitude.

Murder is in the heart before it is in the hand. Therefore, John warns against having the wrong attitude toward others. Hatred has no place in the Christian's heart— toward another Christian brother or any other person for that matter (v. 12).

We should not "marvel" or wonder without understanding if the world hates us (v. 13). The Christian's life is a judgment against the world. For this reason the world hates him. This thought in verse 12 echoes Jesus' words in John 15:18-25.

In the Sermon on the Mount, Jesus went behind the act of murder to the attitude (Matt. 5:21-22). Likewise, John deals with attitudes (1 John 3:14-15). Positively, he says that we know for a certainty *(oida)* that we have passed out of death into life because we "keep on loving" (present

tense) the brethren or our Christian brothers. The one
not loving his brethren continues to abide in death (spiritual death).

Two men were talking about another man. One said, "I
do not like him." In surprise the other said, "I did not
know that you knew him." "I don't," said the other. "If I
knew him I probably would like him." But *love* must go
beyond *liking;* we are to love as Jesus loves. And He loves
all people. You may not *like* a person, but you are to *love*
him. Again Jesus said, "For if ye love them which love
you, what reward have ye? do not even the publicans the
same?" (Matt. 5:46). So our love in Christ must reach out
beyond our own *kind* to include all. Our love is to be given
equally, regardless of class, race, or national origin. Para-
phrasing the words of the poet, if someone draws a circle
about himself to shut you out, you must draw a larger
circle to take him in.

In verse 15 John equates hatred with murder. A person
who hates his brother is a murderer. It is only a matter of
degree. And if hatred persists, more likely than not it will
produce the terrible overt act. How many have you *mur-
dered* through hatred in your heart? Tersely, John says, "No
murderer hath eternal life abiding in him" (v. 15). This
does not mean that a murderer cannot be saved through
faith in Christ. The point here is not so much the overt
act of murder as it is the hatred which John equates with
murder.

(3) *The love of God (3:16-18)*—We know that God
loves us because Christ died for us (v. 16). "Perceive"
renders a perfect tense of the word for experiential knowledge. Notice that in the King James Version "of God" is in
italics, showing that it is not in the Greek text which
simply reads "the love." Johns writes about a specific love,

a love without any modification. "We have learnt to know what love is from this—that Christ laid down his life on our behalf" (TCNT). This is the supreme expression of love.

The Greek reads "he for us his life he laid down." "For" *(huper)* means on behalf of, as a substitute for. This is the only time this word appears in 1 John, although it is common in the Gospel of John. Of course, our laying down our lives cannot save another person. But it is evidence of our own salvation, because we love as God loves. The love so described is a selfless love, as when we forget self on behalf of other Christian brethren.

In verses 17-18 John shows how that we cannot express this love with mere words, but with deeds. The prospect of having to lay down one's life for the brethren, as Christ had done, was a present reality in John's day. Although it is not likely today, in a crisis one might perform such a heroic deed. However, the test of love goes beyond that, in that it is seen in the more ordinary moments of life—for instance, that of helping the needy.

Verse 17 reads like a passage from James (see 2:15-16). If you see someone in need and have the means to supply that need, but do not respond to meet it, John asks, "How dwelleth the love of God in him [you]?" "Good" renders the word *bios,* that which sustains physical life. "See" means more than merely to look at someone. It translates *theōreō* from which comes "theater." It denotes a sustained look, such as one looking at a stage drama. The aorist tense of "shutteth" may read "slams the door". He does not simply look the other way in hope that the needy one will go away. So he deliberately slams the door on his compassion. How could such a person possibly have God's love abiding in him? John appeals to his "little children"

The Children of God

to love more than in word or tongue, but also in deed and in truth (see v. 18). A slap on the back and a "God bless you" will not feed hungry stomachs or clothe cold bodies. If we have the ability to help, however meagerly, and do not do so, such acts and words are sheer hypocrisy. Christians should not be guilty of such.

**(4) The assurance of love (3:19-24)**—Vaughan (pp. 85-86) notes the difficulties faced by interpreters of verses 19-20. But the message comes through in the King James Version. In any case the theme of this passage is assurance before God.

Perhaps the example in verse 20 disturbs us as John's readers. Our failures in righteousness rise up to haunt us, to accuse us before our consciences. Even when true Christians fail, the devil puts into their minds the question: "Would a Christian do as you have done? Surely you are not a Christian." But for the Christian occasional sins of commission and omission are surface reactions; they do not reflect the deeper nature of the soul.

So in verses 19-20 John gives us the way to "assure" or "reassure" our hearts before God who judges righteously that "we are of the truth." "Hearts" in these verses may well read "consciences."

"Condemn" (v. 20), literally, means "to know against." This verb (*kataginōskō*) occurs only three times in the New Testament (see 1 John 3:21; Gal. 2:11). It means to know something against someone in order to condemn. A sensitive conscience will condemn one to the point that he may question whether or not he is a Christian. We know more about ourselves than does any other human being. And the closer we are to the Lord, the more conscious we are of our sins.

93

But "God is greater than our heart, and knoweth all things" (v. 20). Some interpret this to mean that God's condemnation is even greater than that of the conscience. However, a more likely meaning seems to be (1) that God has known all along that which we are just now finding out, but (2) that His knowledge is tempered with love (see 3:1). God, not the conscience, is the judge. He knows the heart, even if outward deeds are wrong. And as Brooke (p. 98) says, "The accusations of conscience are stilled in the presence of omniscient holiness, which is perfect love."

At the same time we should live so as to have a clear conscience (v. 21). Then we can have "confidence" or "boldness" before God. It suggests frank speech and that we have nothing to hide from God.

Standing before God in such fashion gives assurance that when we pray we will receive that for which we pray (see v. 22). Note that "whatsoever" is without limitation. This is possible only because in keeping His "commandments" and doing those things which please Him, our wills will be blended perfectly with His will. Therefore, we will ask for nothing which is outside His will. This does not mean that for a Christian prayer is a magic lamp which by rubbing we get whatever we wish. That would be contrary to the overall biblical teaching concerning prayer. The ideal stated here is perfect harmony between God's will and ours.

Verse 23 defines God's commandment as twofold: (1) Believe on the name of His Son Jesus Christ; and (2) Love one another. In summary, this is to love God absolutely, and to love our neighbors as ourselves. "Believe" is an aorist tense, a once-for-all event involving faith, trust, and commitment. "Love" is a present tense, a continuing practice. This is the first use of *believing* in the epistle, but it is implied in abiding in Christ. Vaughan (pp. 88-89) says, "We infer from this that there is no true belief in the name of Christ [involving His entire person and redemptive work] apart from love for His people. And there is no true love for His people apart from belief in the name of the Son."

Verse 24 is transitional. It climaxes the discussion of love, and introduces the topic of the Holy Spirit, first mentioned in the letter and discussed further in 4:1-6. Note the mutual abiding of Christ in us and we in Him. He abides in us through the Spirit, whose abiding is God's seal of ownership and guarantee of our salvation (see Eph. 1:13b-14).

When we first believed in Jesus, it was through the Spirit's convicting power and our being born from above by His power. Also, in His continuing presence, we are able to grow into the likeness of Christ. Only in His presence may we come to the place where we can pray, "Not as I will, but as you will." Consequently, God's love for us and our love for Him will be perfected, and we will truly be the children of God.

# SIX

## The Testing Of
## The Spirits

*1 John 4:1-6*

---

Outline

I. The Testing (4:1)
II. The Standard (4:2-3)
III. The Victory (4:4)
IV. The Contrast (4:5-6)

---

Out of the Korean War came the following story. While a sentry was walking his post one night he heard a sound in the darkness, and he challenged, "Halt! Who goes there. Friend or foe?" A voice replied, "Friend!" The sentry said, "Repeat the second verse of the 'Star Spangled Banner.'" The voice said, "But I don't know the second verse." The sentry said, "Advance, friend."

Christians must be on their guard in order to recognize their spiritual friend or enemy. John deals with this matter in 1 John 4:1-6. In these brief verses we come to the heart of John's attack on the false teachers. It is quite clear that he has reference to the Gnostics who claimed to be Christians but who were not.

In 2:18-27 using the figure of "antichrists" the apostle emphasizes their denial of the *deity of Jesus* as God's Son. In 4:1-6 the emphasis is upon those who deny the *human-*

*ity of Christ.* In the former he aimed his guns at the Cerinthian Gnostics; in the latter he trains them upon the Docetic Gnostics.

In interpreting these verses two points should be kept in mind. One is the supercharged, Spirit-filled atmosphere of those early churches. The Holy Spirit not only gave practical guidance in the organizational growth of the churches, but He led in a special way in the hammering out of the doctrinal expression of the Christian faith. The other point is to note the informal nature of the worship services. In such, visiting speakers were often given a hearing, a privilege of which false teachers took advantage to teach their heresies. Perhaps John addresses this situation more than any other. He strongly warns his readers against being misled by these speakers.

## I. The Testing (4:1)

"Beloved, believe not every spirit, but try the spirits whether they are of God: because many false prophets are going out into the world." Note John's tender address again (also 4:7,11). They are "beloved" of both God and John. "Believe not" is a second person plural present imperative form preceded by the negative particle. It is a command (note apostolic authority) to "stop believing." Some were being disturbed, and possibly led astray, by the false teachers. And they are to stop it.

The key word in these verses is "spirit." "Spirit" is related to the gift of the Holy Spirit in 3:24b. "Every" renders *pas* without the definite article, pointing out each one of the whole. The *New English Bible* reflects this: "But do not trust any and every spirit." More than one kind of *spirit* sought to control the minds and hearts of Christians. Instead, they are to "try" the spirits. "Try" is the same form as "believe". (In both cases the verb form could be either indicative or imperative, but the context calls for the latter.) "Try" or "test" renders the verb used for testing metal or anything else to see if it is genuine or false. In Luke 14:19 it is used of proving oxen. In Romans 12:2 it is used of proving the will of God (see 1 Cor. 3:13; 1 Thess. 2:4; 5:21). Vaughan (p. 93) notes that ordinarily this verb carried the idea of expecting a thing tested to be true. However, the very idea of testing demands that one rejects that which does not stand the test.

E. M. Blailock (p. 53) is helpful at this point. He suggests "a good and hopeful aim, a proving with the desire in mind that the object proved may stand the test. We are not to be eager to impute error, to find fault and heresy where none is intended. We are not to apply tests and canons of our own invention, eager to demonstrate that all the rest are wrong, and we alone are right. Too often has orthodoxy shown that spirit [which is not of God], and antagonized where it might have reconciled all testimony to truth by a lamentable lack of love which belies truth quite as vital."

We should not *test* with the idea of "get the trial over so we can hang him." We must measure all elements of one's belief. As we speak the truth we should do so in love. But once error has been proved, it should be eradicated. The true purpose of testing the spirits is to determine whether or not they be "of God" or "out of God." The plural "spirits" shows that more than the Holy Spirit is at work in the world. Whereas the Holy Spirit is the Spirit of truth (John 14:17a), the spirit of the devil is that of falsehood

(John 8:44). Jesus said that those who serve the latter will "deceive the very elect" (Matt. 24:24).

Plummer (pp. 94-95) says that this verse "shews us in what spirit to judge such things as the reported miracles of Lourdes and the so-called 'manifestations' of Spiritualism. When if they have been proved to be real, they must still further be proved to see 'whether they are of God.' We are not to judge of doctrine by miracles, but miracles by doctrine. A miracle enforcing what contradicts the teaching of Christ and His apostles is not 'of God' and is no authority for Christians."

The need for testing the spirits is "because many false prophets are gone out into the world." We find many of what John calls *pseudoprophētai* in the Old Testament. Jesus' warning against them (Matt. 7:15; 24:11,24; Mark 13:22) is echoed throughout the New Testament. The word rendered "prophet" may mean either a foreteller or a forth-teller. In the Old Testament prophets did foretell the future, but they also told forth God's message to their contemporaries. In the New Testament their major role was that of a preacher or teacher (but see Acts 11:27-29). A true prophet was one speaking under the direction of the Holy Spirit. False prophets pretended to speak by the Holy Spirit, when in reality they spoke by an evil spirit. There were many false prophets in the world then and each generation since has had them, even as they are with us now.

## II. The Standard (4:2-3)

The standard by which the spirits are to be tested is whether or not they recognize and teach that Jesus Christ

99

is the incarnate Son of God. Paul in 1 Corinthians 12:3 says that "no man speaking by the Spirit of God calleth Jesus accursed: and . . . no man can say that Jesus is the Lord, but by the Holy Ghost [Spirit]." "Jesus accursed" translates *Anathema Iēsous* and "Jesus is Lord" renders *Kurios Iēsous. Anathema* referred to anything so despicable and vile that its utter destruction brought glory to God.

John's standard is similar to Paul's. John says, "Hereby [*en toutōi*, in this] know ye the Spirit of God" (4:2a). "Know," like "believe" and "try" in verse 1, may be either an indicative or an imperative form, that is, it may state a fact or give a command. In this context the indicative seems to be preferred because the point is how to distinguish between the Holy Spirit and the Satanic spirit.

What is the standard? It is that "every spirit that confesseth that Jesus Christ is come in the flesh is of God" (v. 2b). Any prophet who teaches this is "out of God." The Greek reads "in flesh." Christ did not come "into" the flesh of Jesus. The Cerinthian Gnostics taught that Christ was neither born nor did He die; instead, He came upon the man Jesus at His baptism and left Him on the cross. Had John used "into" (*eis*) he would have agreed with the Gnostics. So he carefully chose "in" (*en*). On the other hand, the Docetic Gnostics held that Christ only seemed to have a real flesh and blood body. John refutes their position by saying that Christ came "in" flesh. He had a real flesh and blood body.

Throughout 1 John "Christ" is not used simply as a title such as the Messiah of the Old Testament. "Christ" denotes His deity as the preexistent one (John 1:1) who came in flesh as Jesus of Nazareth the "Son of God" (John 1:14). Hence the name "Jesus Christ." "In flesh" speaks of His nature wherein He completely identified Himself with men, apart from sin. "Is come" is a perfect tense, showing that the identity of Christ with Jesus is an abiding reality, not a temporary relationship. Moffatt reads, "Every spirit which confesses Jesus as the Christ incarnate comes from God."

Conversely, "every spirit that confesseth not that Jesus Christ is come in the flesh is not of God" (v. 3a). In the best manuscripts the reading is simply "who does not confess Jesus." The rest may be implied from verse 2. But John deliberately used "Jesus" without "Christ" in order to stress His humanity, the human Jesus, whom the Gnostics practically ignored. Because He is God incarnate, not to confess Him as such shows that one is speaking for the evil spirit.

You cannot ignore or deny the full deity of Jesus and also His full humanity without negating God's redemptive work in history. For it was in Him that God accomplished His eternal redemptive purpose. Of interest is the fact that in verse 3a the Greek text reads "the Jesus" or the one mentioned in verse 2. Smith (p. 189) reads it as "the aforementioned Jesus." We may summarize verses 2b-3a thus: the incarnation of Christ as Jesus of Nazareth is not simply the heart of the gospel; it is the gospel. In verse 3b John identifies those who deny Jesus Christ as "that spirit of antichrist" of whom his readers have heard, and who is already at work in the world (see 2:18-23). "Spirit" is in italics in the King James Version, which means that it is not in the Greek text. It reads literally, "And this is the of the antichrist." In other words, such a denial of Jesus is characteristic of the Antichrist. Though such a person will not appear until near the end of the age, he is already at work in the world through *antichrists.* No matter how cultured and learned a person may be, if he denies the deity of Jesus and the humanity of Christ he is to be characterized as an antichrist.


## III. The Victory (4:4)

In their struggle against Gnosticism John encourages his readers that they might continue to resist these false prophets. In doing so he bases his exhortation on three evident truths.

First, "ye are of God, little children." "Ye" is emphatic, separating "little children" from the false teachers. They are reminded of their divine origin: "out of [*ek*] God." Their opponents are not out of God but out of Satan. Christians derive their spiritual being from God, and, therefore, are His true people (see 1 Pet. 2:1-10).

Second, they "have overcome them" or the Gnostics. "Have overcome" is the same verb used by Jesus in John 16:33. It is a perfect tense denoting complete victory. Christ's people will suffer tribulation in this world, but they are to "be of good cheer [courage]." In Christ they also will fully conquer the world. After listing the various adverse things that may befall us, Paul says, "We are more than conquerors through him that loved us" (Rom. 8:37). "More than conquerors" renders *hupernikōen*, over and above conquerors or super-conquerors. The basic verb is the same one used in John 16:33 and 1 John 4:4, but in Romans it has the prefix *huper*.

Third, the basis of their victory is the indwelling Christ through the Holy Spirit. "Because greater is he that is in you, than he that is in the world." Here "world" is used as a synonym for Gnosticism. It is a social order that gives no recognition to God. The one in the Christians is God; the one in the Gnostics is Satan. Even though Satan may rage and rant, victory belongs to God and His people.

## IV. The Contrast (4:5-6)

In these verses John concludes his discussion of testing the spirits by drawing a contrast between false and true teachers. This is seen in the emphatic use of "they" (v. 5) and "we" (v. 6). "They" refers to the false teachers of Gnosticism. Since they are "out of the world," they keep on speaking out of worldly wisdom; and the world "keeps on hearing them" (*akouō*, present tense).

Smith (p. 190) points out that the verb for "speak" is not *legō*, "to speak," but *laleō*, "to talk" (v. 5b). This suggests prating, or talking without sense or meaning and/or to talk boastfully. He adds, "The world listens to those who speak its own language." False teachers may attract large crowds, but the size of the crowd does not necessarily mean that one is preaching the gospel. Because the world goes to hear what it wants to hear anyway, it is no compliment to a preacher to say, "He speaks our language." It is condemnation when the world says, "He is one of us" or "He is my kind of preacher."

Of course, the fact that a person draws large crowds does not necessarily mean that he is a false teacher. Some people like to hear the gospel. The difference between true and false teachers is in their message. But it is sad that heretics always seem to have a following.

On the other hand, the Christian teachers ("we") are "out of God" (v. 6). They get their inspiration and message from Him, and "are in tune with the infinite God" (Robertson, p. 231). For this reason those who "know"

God hear them. "Know" renders a present participle of the verb "to know by experience." The participle carries the idea of "are getting to know God by continuous experience." The Christian life is a pilgrimage, which begins by coming to know God through a personal experience with Christ, and continuing toward a greater experiential knowledge of Him. What a joy it is to teach and preach such a message!

Conversely, those who are not "out of God" do not hear His messengers. John is not thinking of the lost person who is seeking God. He has in mind those who are so wedded to the world that they reject the truth. Like every true herald of God, John had felt their cold, icy stares as his words bounced off of crusted consciences and hardened hearts.

One word of caution is needed here. Whereas John spoke with apostolic authority, we should be careful as individual Christians not to adopt the position that everyone who does not agree with us is of the devil. The focal point is not the speaker but the message. The message authenticates the speaker, not the speaker the message. Only as God's truth is declared can John's position be true for us. Furthermore, we should heed Paul's words about speaking the truth in love (Eph. 4:15a). Speaking the truth without love may drive away the hearer rather than draw him to Christ.

Verse 6b summarizes the thought in verses 5-6a. It is thus that we may recognize or test the spirits. Here the reading should be "the Spirit of truth" (John 14:17), instead of "spirit" in lower case. Interpreters generally agree that "the spirit of truth" is the Holy Spirit and "the spirit of error" is Satan. Only here in the New Testament do we find "the spirit of error" *(to pneuma tēs planēs).*

However, in 1 Timothy 4:1 we find "seducing spirits" *(pneumasin planois)* or "misleading spirits." The sense is the same.

John not only commands that we "try the spirits," but he also tells us how. In 1 Corinthians 12:10 Paul lists "discerning of spirits" or "judging the spirits" as a gift of the Holy Spirit. However, here John implies that every Christian has the ability to test the spirits. By being on the alert in order to separate the true from the false, Christians will save the body of Christ from much agony and conflict.

# SEVEN
# The Glory
# Of Love

*1 John 4:7–5:3*

---

### Outline

---

Early one morning Mrs. Hobbs and I flew from Rome, Italy to Zurich, Switzerland. The previous night a heavy snowstorm had covered the Alps in a blanket of white. As far as our eyes could see in all directions there was not one dark spot to mar its beauty, only that here and there a lofty peak towered above the mountains. In the early morning sunlight the entire panorama sparkled as one gigantic diamond. As we gasped at this beautiful sight I thought of the purity of God's love which covers the entire earth. If His love had its way the whole world would sparkle in the sunlight of His smile. The entire Bible is the Word of God. But in this *mountain range* of divine revelation are lofty peaks which tower above all else. Some of these "peaks" are Psalm 23; Isaiah 53; John 1:1-14; 14-17; 1 Corinthians 13, and the passage before us. It glorifies God's love for us, the Christian's love for Him, and our love for each other. As one has said, John turns love about like a brilliant diamond, permitting various angles of light to flash upon it. Thus we see that love is the most beautiful and grandest thing in the world.

## I. The Basis of Love (4:7-12)

In 1 John the verb for *love* (*agapaō*) is used twenty-eight times. The noun (*agapē*) is found eighteen times; the adjective "beloved" (*agapētos*) appears five times. The Greek language has three basic words for love: *philia, eros,* and *agapē*. *Philia* denotes the warm love of friendship. It appears only one time in the New Testament (James 4:4). *Philos* (friend) appears twenty-nine times, and the verb (*phileō*) is used twenty-five times. *Eros* (note "erotic") for the most part connotes sexual desire. It is not found in the New Testament.

In non-biblical Greek *agapē* was regarded as a cold word, in contrast to the warmth of *philia*. Therefore, *agapē* is used very little outside the Bible. Vaughan (p. 109) notes that it was practically unknown outside the Scriptures. By contrast *philia* and its cognates were used abundantly.

For this reason it is interesting to note that the reverse is true in the New Testament. *Philia* and its cognates appear only fifty-five times; but *agapē* and its cognates are found three hundred and twenty times: *agapē* (noun, 116), *agapaō* (verb, 142), and *agapētos* (adjective, 62). It would appear, therefore, that because of the very scarcity of these words in non-biblical Greek, the Holy Spirit chose *agapē* to express the highest kind of love. *Agapē* expresses absolute loyalty to its object. As previously noted, W. Hersey Davis said that "selflessness" best translates it. As sin is selfishness, *agapē* love is selflessness.

1. The source of love (4:7-10)

In keeping with the theme of this passage John again addresses his readers as "beloved" (*agapētoi*, plural, v. 7). He repeats the essence of the old-new commandment as he exhorts his little children to love one another. The reason being that "the love is out of God" as its source (see v. 10). So that every one who has this love as a way of life "is born of God, and knoweth God." "Is born" is a perfect passive form, "has been born out of God," which expresses a completed action. "Knoweth" is a present tense, "keeps on knowing God." Robertson (p. 232) says "is acquainted with God" (see Vaughan, p. 103), but Smith (p. 191) gives an added thought: "by the practice of love they 'get to know God' more and more." Blaise Pascal said, "Human things must be known to be loved; but Divine things must be loved to be known."

Conversely, the one not having the habit of loving, "knoweth not God" (v. 8). Here "knoweth" is a timeless aorist form, "never at any time knew God." He has no acquaintance with God or never did get acquainted with Him. One may have gone through the form of professing to have a Christian faith, but *form* alone is insufficient. If the experience is genuine, it will demonstrate itself in the way one lives. Note how John equates *love* with an experiential knowledge of God. He also gives loving one another as evidence of one's genuine knowledge of God. Again Smith (p. 191) makes a telling comment. "A stranger to love is a stranger to God." Why? Because "God is love." The Greek text has the definite article with "God," but not with "love." Therefore, it cannot be translated, "Love is God," but only, "God is love."

This assertion in verse 8 is stronger than the one in verse 7 where love finds its source in God. Verse 8 expresses the very nature of God as love. "God loves" does not simply mean that He creates, judges, and rules; these are only expressions of God's activities. "God is love" expresses fundamentally the very essence of God. Whatever God does He does as an activity of His love or as an expression of His nature. He creates in love, rules in love, and judges in love (see Vaughan, p. 104).

However, we should not build an entire theological system out of this declaration. Theologians list the natural attributes of God such as omnipotence, omniscience, and omnipresence, but all of these are qualified by His love. Love also qualifies His four moral attributes: holiness, righteousness, truth, and love. As such, God loves the sinner but hates sin. So it is incorrect to say that because God is love, He will not judge all that is opposed to His love. Because He is love, God works against whatever works against love.

As stated earlier, every false system of religious thought is the product of emphasizing one facet of God's nature and ignoring all else. Out of such comes the idea that a God of love will not create a soul and then send it to hell. Actually, He sends no one to hell. As *love* He has done all that even God can do to save us from hell. If anyone goes there, he does so of his own choice in rebellion against God's redemptive love as expressed in Christ.

This truth is expressed in verse 9. The incarnation of God in Christ Jesus is the supreme manifestation of His love "that we might live through him" (see Rom. 5:8). Therefore, the miracles of Jesus' virgin birth, sinless life, atoning death, and bodily resurrection are rooted in God's nature or love. Through these acts, the holy, righteous, and true God provides the means whereby lost people may be saved. It does not mean *universalism* or that all people are automatically saved. It means that all *may* be saved through faith in God's "only begotten Son."

"Only begotten" as applied to Christ is peculiar to John (John 1:14,18; 3:16,18; 1 John 4:9). This places God's Son in a class by Himself. Many interpreters insist that "only" without "begotten" is the best translation of the word so rendered. In any case, God gave His unique possession for our sins. Had silver and gold sufficed God could have given tons and tons of it, and still have tons and tons left. But He had only *one Son*. And He gave Him as a redemptive price for our sins (see 1 Pet. 1:18-19)!

Verse 10 forms a fitting climax to this thought about God as love. "Herein" renders "in this." In this one thing do we see *love;* it is not that we love God first. When even a lost person rightly regards all that God does for him providentially, sane human reason tells him that he should love God. God is so good to me that His blessings should evoke my response of love.

The real essence of love is that God loves us. We are so unworthy, so contrary to everything that God is in his nature, that we should not complain if He were utterly repulsed by what and who we are. But God loves us, not for what we are but despite it. He has fully expressed this love by sending His Son as "the propitiation for our sins" (2:2). This means that in the redemptive work of Jesus

Christ, this holy, righteous, and true God has provided the grounds upon which He can forgive our sins without violating His own nature. This is grace. The late C. Roy Angell once said that grace means that God has given to us what we need rather than what we deserve.

2. The demands of love (4:11-12)

Because of God's loving gift of grace, we should respond in kind to his love by loving one another. Note again John's tender address as "beloved"—beloved of God as well as of the apostle.

"If God so loved us" (v. 11a) is a condition assumed as being true. It may well read, "Since God so loved us." "So" renders the same word found in John 3:16 (*houtōs*). It expresses both the manner, degree, and extent of God's love. Note Paul's four dimensions of Christ's love: breadth, length, depth, and height (see Eph. 3:18). Christ's love is as broad as mankind, as long as eternity, as deep as human need, and as high as the highest heaven, the very throne of God. Vaughan (p. 107) sees "so" as both quantitative (so much) and qualitative (in such a manner), with emphasis upon the latter. God's love was given to us not because of our merit but because of our need.

In verse 11b "we" is emphatic. "We on our part ought also to love one another." Because this is a statement of a fact, not merely an exhortation, we are under obligation to love one another as God loved/loves us. Like God's love, our love should be demonstrated in the arena of life. Smith (p. 191) says, "If we are God's children, we must have our Father's spirit." Therefore, we will not simply verbalize our love; we will express it in love-action toward others.

In verse 12 "God" is emphatic. It reads literally, "God

no one at any time has seen." With the exception of the verb this is exactly the wording of John 1:18. In John 1:18 the verb means to see with the natural eye. Here it means to behold as a spectator, or "to contemplate." Both are perfect tenses, so may read "really has seen" or "beheld."

Although no man has seen God in the essence of His deity (natural eyes cannot do so), "if we love one another, God dwelleth in us, and his love is perfected in us." This may have three possible meanings; indeed, it may contain all three: (1) if we love one another, which means that we are in accord with God's will, He indwells us as truly as if we saw Him; (2) since God is invisible, we cannot express our love for Him as to a visible being, but in loving others we love Him; and (3) living a life of love is the way to let others see the invisible God in us. As God once revealed Himself in His Son, He does so now in His people.

Therefore, God's love "is perfected" in us. The perfect tense of the verb so rendered means to accomplish a purpose fully. When we practice brotherly love, the goal of God's love has been fully reached in us. McDowell (p. 217) comments, "The meaning is that God's love is brought to consummation, finds its appropriate expression and end in us. God's love is made real, tangible, concrete in and through the Christian fellowship when the children of God practice love toward one another."

## II. The Mutual Indwelling (4:13-16)

The recurring theme in this section is the intimate relation between God and the believer. In these verses John begins a fuller treatment of this theme which runs through 5:3.

1. The gift of the Spirit (4:13)

How do we know that we are dwelling in God and He in us? It is "because he hath given us of his Spirit." As others see God in us through our love, so God gives us assurance of this mutual indwelling through the presence of His Spirit in us. At the moment we believe in Jesus as our Savior, the Holy Spirit takes up His abode in our lives (see John 14:17; Eph. 1:13b-14).

In Romans 8:15-18 Paul uses the figure of the Roman law of adoption, whereby one was said to be born again into a new family. This legal figure corresponds to Jesus' vital figure of the New Birth (see John 3:3). In the Roman law two witnesses to the transaction were necessary. These two witnesses are seen in Romans 8:16: "The Spirit itself [himself] beareth witness with our spirit, that we are the children of God." Indeed, in Romans 8:9b Paul says, "Now if any man have not the Spirit of Christ, he is none of his." The indwelling Spirit, therefore, is not an *extra* experience coming at a subsequent point in the Christian's life. At the outset, He serves as evidence that we are Christians—that God dwells in us and we in Him.

2. The basis of indwelling (4:14-15)

The basis of this mutual indwelling of God in us and we in Him is our faith in and confession of Jesus Christ as God's Son and our Savior. In verse 14 "we" is emphatic: "We on our part" or "we ourselves." This pronoun refers to the apostolic witness concerning Jesus Christ. It was not based upon hearsay but upon personal experience. "Have seen" is a perfect tense of the verb "to view as a spectator," or a contemplative look. It is the same verb as in verse 12, except there is a difference in person and number—first person plural. The perfect tense expresses not only the certainty of seeing, but that their seeing remains in memory.

"Testify" means not only to bear witness in court, but also to bear witness to Jesus. He had charged his disciples to witness (see Acts 1:8), and that they continue to do it. What is the witness? "That the Father sent the Son to be the Saviour of the world" (v. 14). "Sent" is a perfect indicative form, which means that the event was in the past, but its effect still abides at the time of writing. The action's continuation into the future is also implied.

Now John adds that "whosoever shall confess that Jesus is the Son of God, God dwelleth in him, and he in God" (v. 15). This is the response one must give to the witness mentioned in verse 14. This is another blow at the Gnostics who denied both the humanity of Christ and the deity of Jesus. It is a confession that Jesus is the eternal Son of God. Jesus, who is potentially the Savior of all men, actually becomes the Savior of the one making this confession.

This involves more than the repetition of a creed; it means total commitment to Jesus Christ. To make this confession in John's day meant persecution and, perhaps, death. As one has said, it involved complete separation from one's former community, whether Jew or Gentile. Such a confession would be made only if one saw in Jesus the total answer to his need, and found in His indwelling power the *presence* sufficient for such a need.

"Shall confess" renders an aorist tense, which points to a definite confession. The time is not specified, but the experience is declared as a decisive one at a given point in one's spiritual pilgrimage. Having made the confession, the believer has the assurance that, in His Spirit, God "keeps on abiding" (present tense) in him and he in God.

3. The evidence of indwelling (4:16)

Out of his own experience John assures his readers that what had happened to him and other believers can be the experience of all who believe in Jesus. In this verse "we" is emphatic. Some see it as a reference to the apostles (v. 14), but other scholars include John's readers as well (v. 15). Whether either or both can be true, it is still true of those who in faith commit themselves to Jesus.

Both "have known" and "believed" are perfect tenses. These verbs of completeness add to the emphasis of "we." "Have known" expresses experiential knowledge: "We have come to know by experience and still know, and we have come to believe and still believe." In John 6:69 we have the same verbs only in reverse order. In response to Jesus' question as to whether or not the apostles would join the Galilean crowds in deserting Him, Peter answered, "Lord, to whom shall we go? thou hast the words of eternal life. And we believe and are sure [know] that thou art the Holy One of God" (best Greek texts). Here "we" and "thou" are both emphatic. "We" in contrast to the departing crowd; "you" and no one else.

In John 6:69 *experiential knowledge* came through *faith*. We are not to suppose that in 1 John 4:16 *faith* came through *knowledge*. But the joining of the two words shows their intimate relation in our Christian experience. John Calvin (p. 244) renders this "We have known by believing." Says he, "Such knowledge is not attained but by faith."

That which is known and believed is "the love that God hath to us." However, the Greek text reads *en hēmin,* or "in the sphere of us;" in us God's love is expressed. Some translations read "for us" (RSV, Williams), but both "in us" and "for us" are true. It is God's love *for* us expressed *in* us.

115

By way of summary, John returns to the sublime thought of verse 8: "God is love." For this reason, he concludes that the one abiding in love *(agapē)* abides in God and He in him. All three references to *abide* are present tenses, which implies a continuous state.

## III. The Perfected Love (4:17-5:3)

In verse 12 John has noted that God's love is perfected or reaches its intended goal in our love for each other. Here in 4:17 to 5:3 he begins a more thorough treatment of this perfected love, only here our love is also perfected in its expression to both God and the brethren.

The key phrase in this passage is "Herein [in this] is love perfected with us" (best Greek text). John does not imply that in this life we will achieve perfection, but that our love will achieve its intended goal. This goal is threefold: (1) assurance at the judgment (vv. 17-18); (2) love for the brethren (4:19-5:1); (3) and obedience to God's commandments (5:2-3).

### 1. The assurance at the judgment (4:17-18)

In 1 John 2:28 the word for "boldness" is rendered "confidence," which concerns the Lord's return. In 4:17 "judgment" refers to the final judgment. While it introduces a conclusion based upon God's love for us and our love for Him and our fellow-believers, "herein" actually points toward this final judgment. Love reaches its climax in our boldness or assurance at the final judgment.

The reason for this boldness is that "as he is, so are we in this world." Both "he" and "we" are emphatic, but this does not mean that we will be perfect as God is perfect. It means that we are accepted before Him in Christ (Eph. 1:6). Thus we share in His confidence before the Father. However, to the extent that we love, "we are like him." McDowell (p. 218) calls this a "daring thought!" McDowell also adds, "He abides in us and we in him; we are his children; we love as he loves." That is, to the degree that we love we find the fruition of our relation to Him. Although His love is infinite, it is nonetheless the goal toward which we are to strive. It is in this increasing love that we will find boldness before God in the judgment.

Verse 18 is one of many gems of truth found in this epistle. "There is no fear in love; but perfect love casteth out fear." There is no dwelling place for fear in love. Used in the sense of dread or terror, fear is the opposite of boldness. Boldness is possible because to the degree that we achieve the goal of love, we cast out fear. At the judgment, knowing that God loves us, and we love Him and other people, we will not stand as a guilty criminal before the bar of stern justice. Instead, we will stand before our loving Father who loves to give good gifts to his children.

"Fear hath torment" or punishment. One of two meanings is possible: either fear itself is punishment, or fear grows out of punishment. Although both are true, perhaps the former is to be preferred. In any case one dwelling in fear has not reached the goal of perfect love.

2. The love for the brethren (4:19-5:1)

Humans express the love of God through not only their love for Christian brethren, but also through their attitude toward all men. God does not simply love His friends, but His foes as well. However, His love becomes effective in redemption only for those who respond to His love in faith.

"We love him, because he first loved us" (v. 19). Both "we" and "he" are emphatic. Because love originates with God, from Him comes our ability to love. In *agapē* He is the author and prime mover (McDowell, p. 219). Thus He does not love us in response to our love, but rather, because He first loved us, we respond to His love in faith.

However, John labels anyone a liar who claims to love God, but who hates his brother (v. 20). If our love does not go out to one whom we have seen, how can we love God whom we have not seen? This is a probing question. This question points to our brother as the means of demonstrating our love for God. The Greek text reads, "For the one not having the habit of loving his brother whom he has really seen [perfect tense] with the natural eye, God whom he has not really seen with the natural eye he is not able to love." If my love does not reach next door, it certainly cannot reach up to heaven. Brooke (pp. 125-26) states it thus: love must have an object, and "if it fails to find out the nearer object [our fellows] it will never reach the further [God]". Love for God expresses itself in obedience to God's command that "he who loveth God love his brother also" (v. 21).

Previously, John has spoken of love, sonship, and faith. Now he brings them together, so that you cannot view any one of them in isolation. Anyone who believes that Jesus is the Christ has been born of God, and is, therefore, God's child (5.1).

Unfortunately, no English verb for "faith" corresponds to the Greek *pisteuō*. It is, therefore, usually rendered "believe." This weakens it, in that we associate this word with intellectual assent, whereas *pisteuō* actually means to have faith, to trust, and to commit. This last usage is found in John 2:24: "Jesus did not commit himself unto them, because he knew all men." Of course, one must believe intellectually that "Jesus is the Christ," but this is believing *about* Him. Beyond this one must believe or trust *in* Him, and commit himself to Jesus' will and way.

If we love Him who "begat" we must also love others who are "begotten" of Him. "Every one who loves the parent loves the child" (RSV). So if we love God we will love His children. You may not agree with another Christian, or even like him or his ways. But in the sense of *agapē*, selfless giving of yourself to him, you must love him. We may be certain that in our sins of commission and omission God is not pleased, but He loves us just the same. We must do the same with our brethren.

## 3. The obedience of love (5:2-3)

Already in 4:21 John has noted God's command about love. Now he stresses the relationship between love and obedience. "By this" we know that we love God's children—"when we love God, and keep [do] his commandments" (v. 2). Note the plural "commandments." This goes beyond love for the brethren, but it certainly includes it. A loving child will be an obedient child. We obey, not out of fear, but out of love.

By way of summary John says, "For this is the love of God, that we keep his commandments: and his commandments are not grievous" (v. 3). Someone said, "To love as Christ loves is to let our love be a practical and not a sentimental thing." While we cannot separate love and action, we do not love simply by *doing*. We *do* because we love. One might keep God's laws selfishly with a hope of reward, but this is no proper response to God's love.

Christian love does not ask "must I" but "may I;" it does not count the cost, but weighs the privilege. You may give without loving, but you cannot love without giving.

The apostle adds in verse 3 that God's commandments are not grievous or heavy (cf. Matt. 11:28,30). To the one who loves God they become a joy rather than a burden. Robertson (p. 238) says, "Love for God lightens his commands." God asks us to do what He is doing, which includes love for the brethren.

An old story tells it all. Someone saw a little girl carrying her heavy baby brother on her back. When asked if he was not too heavy a load for her to carry, she replied with a smile, "Oh, no sir! For, you see, he's my brother!"

# EIGHT

# The Victory
# Of Faith

*1 John 5:4-12*

---

Outline

I. The Overcoming Power of Faith (5:4-5)
   1. The principle stated (5:4)
   2. The personal application (5:5)
II. The Object of Faith (5:6)
III. The Verifying Witnesses (5:7-12)
   1. The threefold witness (vv. 7-9)
   2. The experiential witness (v. 10)
   3. The substance of the witness (vv. 11-12)

---

Every person lives by faith. It is all a matter of the object of one's faith. Our son, a chemical engineer, did chemical research for years. One day while we were talking about faith, he said that every research scientist begins with faith. Recognizing that there is something that he does not know, he has faith that by following certain scientific principles in experiments he can learn that which he does not know.

A husband has faith in his wife, or else he would demand a chemical analysis of food she prepared for him, lest she had put poison in it. A soldier at war has faith in his country and its cause. Otherwise he will not risk his life defending them. A merchant has faith in money which he accepts for products he sells. An employee does likewise as he receives money in payment for services rendered.

A new and useful product is discovered. A husband eats and is nourished by food prepared by his wife. A war is won. A nation's economy is sound. Each of these is a victory of faith. If faith plays so vital a part in the more mundane areas of life, it is especially true in spiritual matters. Faith has its victories there also.

## I. The Overcoming Power of Faith (5:4-5)

Even a casual reading of John's writings reveals his great emphasis upon *faith*. Out of more than one hundred times that the Greek verb (*pisteuō*, usually translated "believe") appears in the New Testament, more than half of them appear in the Johannine literature. Interestingly enough, the noun "faith" (*pistis*) is found in his Gospel and epistles only in 1 John 5:4. But this one use is of great significance, for it declares the conquering power resident in faith.

### 1. The principle stated (5:4)

In 5:1 John says that "whosoever believeth that Jesus is the Christ is born of God." He uses the masculine present participle, referring to a person, literally, "every single one believing."

But in verse 4 he uses a neuter perfect passive participle. The perfect tense is the tense of completeness, and expresses a past action which is true in the present, the implication being that it will continue into the future.

The passive voice denotes an act done by another to the subject. Hence it is a complete being born "of God" or "out of God." It is an act performed not by the subject unto himself/itself, but a work of God.

However, the significant thing in this verse is the *neuter* form of the participle: "whatsoever," not "whosoever." It introduces a broad principle rather than a particular incident or person. Williams applies this principle to a person: "Every child of God continues to conquer." Although this is true, Williams narrows the principle stated by John. More aptly Knox catches his meaning: "Whatsoever takes its origin from God must needs triumph over the world." This involves truth as a principle as well as persons who contend for the truth. In the well-known adage, "truth crushed to earth will rise again." Because truth is ultimately victorious, we should never be afraid to allow truth to combat error.

Some people spend their energy and time defending the Bible. What we should do is to proclaim its truth, and it will take care of itself. A yapping poodle may torment a large mastiff dog tied to a post, but the mastiff does not need your protection. Just turn him loose, and he will take care of the situation.

The victory of which John speaks is a continuous one. This is seen in the present tense of "overcometh" (*nika*, keeps on overcoming). "The world" (*ho kosmos*, note "cosmic") refers to all forces which are opposed to spiritual truth. The struggle between truth and falsehood is a constant one. Falsehood may win a temporary skirmish here and there, but in the war the things of God are assured of victory.

John further states the principle that "the victory" is our faith. "Victory" (*nikē*) is the noun form of the verb *nikaō* used in 5:4. Nike was the Greek goddess of victory. Nicopolis means "city of victory," so named by Octavius (Caesar Augustus) to commemorate his victory over Anthony and Cleopatra. In the Louvre in Paris you will see the masterpiece in sculpture called *Nike* or "Winged Victory."

"Overcometh" renders an aorist participle which should be expressed in the past tense "overcame." The primary sense of the aorist tense is the kind of action expressed (point action), called the historical tense. The precise meaning here is not clear, but it could refer to the victory won at the time of one's regeneration (see v. 4a), or to a promise of victory over the Gnostic heretics (see v. 5). Since 1 John was written in the shadow of emperor worship, as plainly presented in Revelation, victory could also be related to the deification of the emperor and the power of the Roman empire. It could also summarize past victories that John's readers had won through faith. However, since verse 4 seems to be the statement of a general principle rather than of specific events (note "whatsoever"), most likely the apostle is simply declaring that the means of spiritual victory is faith.

Since he uses the definite article ("the faith of us"), he means a particular kind of faith. This faith centers in and submits to God the Father and the Lord Jesus Christ. While this faith is identified with victory, actually the power is of God. Faith is the channel through which the power flows.

2. The personal application (5:5)

In verse 5 John is more specific as to "the faith" of verse 4. It is the faith which one has that Jesus is the Son of God. It focuses upon the problem of the Gnostics who denied this relationship between the historical Jesus and God. This is the heart of the Christian faith: Jesus (Humanity) is the Son of God (Deity). The Cerinthian Gnostics denied the deity of Jesus. The Docetic Gnostics denied the humanity of Christ. The one holding to both the diety and the humanity of Christ will be victorious over their heresies.

Significantly, John did not use the word "Christ" here as he did in 5:1. The Gnostics conceived the Christ as the lowest of the created beings emanating from God in an imaginary chain of *aeons*, and therefore, was not deity. However, John in this epistle uses "Christ" and "Son of God" interchangeably. Here John gives a direct unity between the eternal *Son* and the historical *Jesus*. Such a faith was victorious over the Gnostics then; it is victorious over neo-Gnostics now, and in wrestling with all other spiritual problems. Thus John's general principle applies today as it did in the first century. It is both timely and timeless.

## II. The Object of Faith (5:6)

Having shown generally that "Jesus is the Son of God," John proceeds to identify Him more specifically. He definitely has the Gnostic heresy in mind at this point.

In his use of "came" John clearly relates this statement to the gospel record and the prophetic tradition. Literally, the text reads, "the one coming" or "the coming one." The aorist participle points to a historical event which took place, hence the past tense "came."

Reflecting their messianic hope the Jews referred to the Messiah as "the Coming One" (see Mal. 3:1, "he shall come"). This hope is seen in the Gospels as a technical term for the Messiah as fulfilled in Jesus (see Matt. 11:3; 23:39; John 3:31; 6:14; 11:27; 12:13). In verse 6 John declares that He has already come. "Came" may be seen as a synonym for "Christ."

What does he mean "by [*dia*, through) water and blood?" Various suggestions have been made. For instance, the ordinances of baptism and the Lord's Supper, or the phenomenon of blood mingled with water when the soldier pierced the side of Jesus' dead body on the cross. But neither of these seems likely.

We must remember the immediate context of this statement. John is writing to refute the Gnostic heresy. The Docetics denied the humanity of Christ, that is, that He did not have a real flesh and blood body, but only *seemed* (from *dokeō*, I seem) to have. The Cerinthians denied the deity of Jesus. They held that the aeon Christ came upon Him at His baptism (Matt. 3:16) and left Him on the cross (Matt. 27:46); Christ neither was born nor did He die. According to the Cerinthians only the man Jesus was born by natural means, and died, which left their system devoid of God's redemptive purpose and work. It involved "water" (baptism) but not "blood."

John declares that He "came by [through] water and blood, even Jesus Christ." Note both the human and divine names. Through His baptism Jesus consecrated Himself to His mission, and through His blood He consummated it. Then John adds "not by water only, but by water and blood." The apostle includes both by way of an emphatic statement. In the Greek text both "water" and "blood" have the definite article, making them separate events. The one came at the beginning of His ministry; the latter at its close. By these John offers proof that Jesus

Christ is the Son of God. Thus the aorist tense of "came" may be seen as inclusive of the entire public ministry of Jesus.

To understand John's meaning in "water" we must recall, as apparently he did, the words of John the Baptist: "And I knew him not, but he that sent me to baptize with [*en*, in] water, the same said unto me, Upon whom thou shalt see the Spirit descending, and remaining on him, the same is he which baptizeth with the Holy Ghost [Spirit]. And I saw, and bare record that this is the Son of God" (John 1:33–34).

McDowell (p. 222) says, "The water testifies to the fact that Jesus was a true historical being who joined hands with his forerunner John the Baptist in providing the historical event of his baptism, evidence that he was the Messiah of prophecy. The witness of the Spirit to the messiahship of Jesus was first given at the baptism, but it was a continuing witness in the work and words of Jesus and in the work and witness of all believers."

Notice that the Baptist did not say that He "will be" or "will become" the Son of God, but that "this is the Son of God." The verb "to be" expresses essential being. In the case of Jesus it is eternal essential being (see John 1:1,14). The apostle does not imply that Jesus was not God's Son prior to His baptism. He means that this fact was revealed to John the Baptist on this occasion, who, in turn, bore witness to his hearers. It is the responsibility of Jesus' followers to pass it on to those who have not heard.

John 1:14 adds the apostle's comment, "And we beheld his glory, the glory as of the only begotten of the Father, full of grace and truth." This refers not simply to Jesus' transfiguration, but to the whole of His ministry among men, which further testifies of Christ's historical reality.

"The blood," of course, refers to Jesus' death on the cross. His death speaks of His identity with mankind, apart from sin. Blood represents life. In giving His blood He gave His life. Also blood shows that Christ did possess a body of flesh and blood, and that He died for man's sins. Truly, "God was in Christ [Jesus], reconciling the world unto himself" (2 Cor. 5:19). The witness concerning Jesus is of the Holy Spirit who is the Spirit of truth.

## III. The Verifying Witnesses (5:7-12)

In these verses John bolsters his statement in verse 6. After showing that gospel history points to Jesus Christ as the object of our faith, he points out repeatedly the firm basis of this faith.

### 1. The threefold witness (vv. 7-9)

In the oldest and best manuscripts the passage "in heaven . . . in earth" (vv. 7-8, KJV) does not appear. The better reading lists the three witnesses of verse 6, but it gives "the Spirit" (RSV) before "the water, and the blood." The Holy Spirit of truth (see John 14:17a) bears witness to Jesus who is *Truth*, (see John 14:6).

The mention of the Spirit before the water and the blood shows that He is the source of the witness concerning Jesus as the Christ. Through them the Holy Spirit confirms the truth alluded to by John. The apostle is not simply giving his own opinion or interpretation of the events. Indeed, the anointing of Jesus by the Spirit at His baptism was accompanied by the approving voice of the Father (Matt. 3:16-17). In the baptismal scene we see the presence of Father (voice), Son (Jesus), and Spirit (dove) at the inauguration of Jesus' public ministry. A later scribe, wanting to interpret Jesus' baptism, added "the Father, the Word, and the Holy Ghost [Spirit]" in 1 John 5:7. The same three persons of the Godhead were present at the crucifixion, which was in accord with the Father's redemptive will (see Matt. 17:5). Through the eternal Spirit (see Heb. 9:14), Jesus went to the cross.

However, John's emphasis is upon the threefold witness of the Spirit, water, and blood. The Mosaic law required two or three witnesses in order to establish a fact in legal proceedings (Deut. 17:6; Matt. 18:16; John 8:17), hence, John's reference to three witnesses.

"And these three agree in one" (5:8). None of the three gave conflicting testimony, or literally, "and the three are unto one." "Unto" *(eis)* may be seen as pointing toward a goal. Three separate witnesses, but they converge into one truth: that Jesus Christ is the Son of God. Verse 7a may be translated, "Because there are three, the ones bearing witness." "Bearing witness" renders a present participle, which means, "they keep on bearing witness down the ages."

The "if" clause in verse 9 assumes that the statement is true. Moffatt reads, "If we accept human testimony." Vaughan (p. 123) catches the sense of it: "If we receive [as we do] the witness of men, the witness of God is greater." So John argues from the lesser to the greater. Surely, then, we should accept God's testimony concerning His Son rather than man's. Brooke (p. 137) sums up the matter: "If we accept the testimony of men when it satisfies the conditions of evidence required by law, much more are we bound to accept the witness which we possess in this case, for it is witness borne by God Himself." To deny the eternal Sonship of Christ is to deny the word of God!

2. The experiential witness (v. 10)

An opponent may argue convincingly against your logic, but he cannot do so against your experience. There is a world of difference between "I think" or "I reason" and "I know." Everyone who has had a personal experience of faith in Jesus Christ as his Savior *knows* that He is God's Son, powerful to save.

Thus John says, literally, "The one believing on the Son of God keeps on having the witness in himself" (v. 10). The witness within himself is the witness of the indwelling Holy Spirit. He gives the believer a sense of new purpose in life, a steadfast assurance for time and eternity, and peace which surpasses human understanding.

Believing involves more than intellectual assent to a truth. The Greek word denotes total faith, trust, and commitment to the redemptive will and work of God through His Son Jesus Christ. Failure to believe is more than mere words. Because "the one not believing God completely makes [perfect tense] him a liar." God has "fully testified" (v. 9b) and "fully borne witness" (v. 10c) that Jesus Christ is His Son. Both verbs are perfect tenses of completeness: His witness was given in the past and still stands. It is upon such testimony that the believer rests his faith.

3. The substance of the witness (vv. 11-12)

These verses summarize John's thoughts about the witness concerning Jesus Christ, the heart of the gospel. Several definite things are said about the substance of the witness.

First, God has given to us *eternal life* (v. 11b). "Life" (*zōē*) denotes spiritual life or salvation life. It is not a life which the believer receives at death and which lasts in eternity. Rather, it is a quality of life which one receives the moment he believes in Jesus, and which abides in eternity. Only God is eternal, and this life is that of God which He imparts to all believers (see John 1:12; 3:16).

Second, God *gave* this eternal life to us. It is not the result of our merit but of God's grace. "Hath given" is an aorist tense of point action, which denotes the point in time when God made this gift. Some see this time as a reference to the incarnation of Christ as Jesus of Nazareth; others see it as the moment of the believer's regeneration. Actually both are true. Since "this life is in his Son," God gave it in the person of Jesus Christ. And it becomes the individual's possession the moment he believes in Jesus as Savior.

Third, the one having the Son has life (v. 12). This is stating in simple terms the idea in the above sentence. "In him was life, and the life was the light of men" (John 1:4). "In him" is emphatic: "In him and in no one else always was light, and the life always was the light of men." John 1:9 reads, literally, "That was the true Light which lighteth every man, coming into the world." And John 1:12 reads, "But as many as received him, to them gave he power to become the sons of God." "Power" renders *exousia* which means "out of being." He imparted to the believer of His very nature, the very life of God Himself.

Fourth, the one not having the Son does not have life. "Have" is a present tense: "keeps on not having life." As one has said, a "Sonless life" is bereft of spiritual life. A man may be a good husband, father, and neighbor and still be dead in sin (see Eph. 2:1); he is not a Christian (see Acts 4:12). It is by God's grace through our faith in His Son that His life flows into us.

Thus faith in Jesus Christ is the faith which enables us

to overcome the world, faith that He is both human and divine, that as Deity-Humanity, He perfectly represents both God and man. In Jesus Christ, God and man meet in reconciliation, and this is the greatest victory of all.

# NINE

# The "Blessed Assurance" Of Believers

*1 John 5:13-21,*

---

Outline

I. The Certainty of Eternal Life (5:13)
II. The Privilege of Prayer (5:14-17)
  1. The confidence in God's promise (vv. 14-15)
  2. The obligation of intercession (vv. 16-17)
III. The Victory Over Sin (5:18)
IV. The Newness of Life (5:19)
V. The Christian's Relation to God (5:20)
VI. The Closing Exhortation (5:21)

---

One of the most thrilling stories of the 1970's was the television program "Roots." It is the story of Alex Haley's search to know whence he came. As the story led us back through the dark era of slavery in America to discover Mr. Haley's origins in Africa, it caught the imagination of an entire nation, yes, of the whole world.

However, the most thrilling story of the ages is that through His Son Jesus Christ, God has provided redemption for all who believe in Him. Thus every believer knows, not simply whence he/she came, but whither he/she is going eternally! We sing of it as

Blessed assurance, Jesus is mine!
Oh, what a foretaste of glory divine!
Heir of salvation, purchase of God,
Born of His Spirit, wash'd in His blood.
—Fanny J. Crosby.

And this "blessed assurance" is a present possession of every Christian, both now and in the endless future.

## I. The Certainty of Eternal Life (5:13)

Verses 13-21 are a summary of the entire epistle. "These things that I have written unto you" refer immediately to 5:1-12, but in a larger sense relate to the main theme which runs throughout the letter.

In John 20:31 John states the primary purpose of his Gospel: "That ye might believe that Jesus is the Christ, the Son of God; and that believing ye might have life through his name." Now in 1 John, which may be seen as his *mini-Gospel*, the apostle says, "These things have I written unto you that believe on the name of the Son of God; that ye may know that ye have eternal life" (v. 13a). The remainder of verse 13 (KJV) is not found in the oldest manuscripts (see RSV). As previously noted "eternal life" (*zōē aiōnios*) is a quality of life which is the believer's present possession and which extends into eternity.

The key word in verses 13-21 is "know." In verse 20b it translates *ginōskō* which means to know by experience. Six times "know" renders *oida*, an experiential knowledge perceived or seen through to the point that it becomes a conviction of the soul. Robertson (p. 242) defines it as knowing with settled intuitive knowledge. Vaughan

(p. 127) points out that the former appears in 1 John twenty-five times; the latter fifteen times.

Therefore, one of the blessed assurances of the Christian is the conviction in his soul that he has age-abiding life. Paul used *oida* in 2 Timothy 1:12: "For I know [in] whom I have believed, and am persuaded that he is able to keep [guard] that which I have committed unto him against that day." Both "believed" and "persuaded" are perfect tenses of completeness, that is, he believed in Jesus Christ, and continues to do so. He has an abiding and fixed persuasion that he is saved and safe.

By reading a bank's financial statement you may conclude that the bank is safe, but that is only believing about it. You believe in it when you deposit your money in it. You may believe everything that the Bible says *about* Jesus. You believe *in* him when you give yourself to him in personal commitment and trust. John assumes that his readers have done the latter. For this reason they have full assurance of eternal life. And what he said to his initial readers he says to all readers through the centuries.

## II. The Privilege of Prayer (5:14-17)

Prayer, both a privilege and an obligation, is the direct line of communication between the soul and God. It is also the means by which we lift to Him our burdens concerning both ourselves and others. As children of God we approach Him directly, without the aid of any other person or thing.

What a privilege it would be if each of us had a direct *hot line* into the Oval Office at the White House, so that when we dial the one answering would be the President of the United States himself. Every believer in Christ has such a line to the throne of grace, and the one who answers the call is our Heavenly Father.

## 1. The confidence in God's promise (vv. 14-15)

The privilege of prayer is all the more sweet because of the "confidence" (v. 14) which we have "in him" [God]. "In" translates *pros*, before, or "face to face" with God. When we talk with someone we do so face to face. We do not stand before God in fear or uncertainty as a slave before his owner, but in confidence as a child before his Father. "Confidence" may also read "boldness" (see 2:28, ASV; "unshaken confidence" Williams).

What is this confidence? It is, "if we ask any thing according to his will, he heareth us." The "if" clause expresses a condition that is not fulfilled, but which may be. It relates to the matter of our asking, not to God's hearing. A petition outside God's will is not really a prayer in the purest sense. Jesus, who prayed in accord with His Father's will, taught His followers to pray in His name, which means on the basis of His merit and in keeping with His will.

"Heareth" is a present indicative form, a declaration of the fact that God always hears when we pray in keeping with His will. Someone says, "I prayed to God, and He did not hear me." What he means is that he did not receive what he wanted. God did hear, but His response is another matter. That is in keeping with His love, will, and wisdom.

The "if" clause in verse 15 is considered a fulfilled condition. Assuming that we "know" (*oidamen*) that God hears us when we pray, we "know" (*oidamen*) that "we have the petitions that we desired [asked] of him." However, this is still qualified by "according to his will." The Christian who has such a faith prays unselfishly that God's will may be done. He is so caught up in God's purposes that he prays according to God's will. John does not say that we necessarily receive the *thing* for which we prayed, but that God responds to our *petitions*. Through experience the Christian knows that if God does not grant the thing for which he asks, He gives something far better.

God has three answers to prayer: yes, no, and wait. He may say "yes" or "no" immediately, but more often than not he says, "Wait." We must wait until we are capable of using properly the thing granted. The old illustration is still true. If a small boy asks his father for a shotgun, out of love and wisdom the father does not say "yes" or "no." He says, "Son, you are not ready to use a shotgun properly. *Wait* until you are, and then I will give one to you."

At times we ask God for things which would be harmful to us and/or others. If we could see into the future we would thank him for saying "no," or as the Bard wrote:

> We, ignorant of ourselves, beg often our own harms,
> Which the wise powers deny our good;
> So we find profit by losing our prayers.
> —William Shakespeare (Antony and Cleopatra,
> Act II, Sc. 1, Line 5)

But when we pray in God's will,

> Our vows are heard betimes! And Heaven takes care
> To grant, before we can conclude the prayer:
> Preventing angels met it half way,
> And sent us back to praise, who came to pray.
> —John Dryden (*Britannia Rediviva*, Line 1).

137

2. The obligation of intercession (vv. 16-17)

Following his assurance of God hearing and granting prayer within His will, John proceeds to enjoin his readers with regard to intercessory prayer. Christians are under obligation to pray for each other.

In verse 16a the apostle envisions a Christian literally seeing "his brother sinning a sin." Rather than to gossip to others about it, he is to ask God to forgive the sinning brother and give him strength to cease it. In such case he is assured that God will forgive him and *revive* him. Of course, forgiveness is dependent upon the sinning Christian's repentance and confession (see 1 John 1:9). As we have seen, Christians do not make sinning their life style. Failure to repent would be evidence that the one sinning is probably a "brother" in name only and not a Christian.

This promise is based upon the assumption that it is a sin "not unto death." For John says, "There is a sin unto death," a mortal or deadly sin. The verb "is" opens the sentence, so it is emphatic. "There *is* a sin unto death." What John means by this is the subject of debate among interpreters. Some see this as a specific sin such as adultery, blasphemy, or murder (see Lev. 20:10), but we know that adultery (David) and murder (Moses) are forgiveable sins. Others regard it as willfully persistent sin or a state, such as in The *New English Bible* which reads, "deadly sin." Probably, John has in mind the unpardonable sin mentioned by Jesus in Matthew 12:31-32. The Pharisees had so persisted in their opposition to Jesus that they had lost the ability to distinguish between good and evil. To an obviously good work of the Holy Spirit they attributed an evil spirit (see Matt. 12:22-37).

In the immediate context John evidently has in mind

the Gnostics. They had persistently resisted the Holy Spirit's revelation concerning Jesus as the Son of God. They denied both His deity and humanity, and instead regarded Him as a demigod, or almost an evil being who created evil matter. Because they had reached the *point of no return* spiritually, the apostle does not command that one should not pray for them. He simply says, "I do not say that he shall pray for it" (v. 16). He makes the general statement that "all unrighteousness is sin, and [but] there is a sin not unto death" (v. 17).

McDowell (p. 223) is helpful at this point. John points out that we should pray for a "brother" whose sin is not mortal. He excludes Christians from those who commit a "sin unto death," the "antichrists" or Gnostics. His point in not praying for them is that it would be fruitless. But he does not mean that we should not pray for unregenerate people as such. We should pray for them, and leave the results with God.

## III. The Victory Over Sin (5:18)

The third blessed assurance of the Christian is that of victory over sin. John does not say that the one born of God does not sin at all. Had this been his thought he would have used the aorist tense of point action: "never at any time sins." The verb "sinneth" is present tense of linear or repeated action: he does not keep on sinning or have the habit of sinning.

"We know" renders *oidamen* (first person plural of *oida*; see vv. 19-20a). This triple use of the verb is most meaningful. "We know perceptively" or with soul conviction. It allows room for no doubt. How does the Christian know this? Because "He that is begotten of God [Jesus Christ] keeps on keeping him." This, not "himself," is the reading of the best texts. The Christian cannot "keep himself;" it is an act of God's Son through God's grace. Through His Spirit (see Rom. 8:9) Christ indwells the Christian (see John 14:17). The verb rendered "keepeth" also means to guard or to stand guard like a sentry walking his post. So Christ stands guard over His own (see John 17:11-12,15; Rev. 3:10; see *Theological Dictionary of the New Testament,* Vol. VIII, pp. 140-143). In 1 John 5:18 "the reference is to the protection against the Devil and sin which is granted by Christ as the Son of God and by the life in the Spirit which He makes possible."

For this reason "that wicked one toucheth him not." "That wicked one" (*ho ponēros,* masculine gender) is "the evil one" (RSV). The definite article points to a particular evil one, Satan. "Touchest" is a present tense: "keeps on not touching him," or, "to lay hold or to grasp." Here the present tense carries the thought of clinging (see John 20:17 which should read, "Stop clinging to me"). Satan repeatedly tries to lay hold upon the Christian, but to do so he must defeat Christ, an impossibility.

This type of security suggests Jesus' words in John 10:28-29. "I give them [his sheep] eternal life; and they shall never perish, neither shall any man [anyone] pluck [snatch] them out of my hand. My Father, which gave them me, is greater than all; and no man [nothing] is able to pluck [snatch] them out of my Father's hand." "Never" translates a strong double negative, "not never perish." In English a double negative makes a positive; in Greek it strengthens the negative idea.

Many people hesitate to trust in Jesus out of fear that

they cannot *hold out.* The blessed truth is that we are not holding on to God; He is holding on to us. In that sublime truth is our assurance of victory over sin.

## IV. The Newness of Life (5:19)

This verse contains two definite statements which we note in reverse order. "The whole world lieth in wickedness" or "the evil one." "Wickedness" renders a masculine form as in verse 18, so it is translated "the evil one" or Satan. "Lieth" (present tense) expresses a continuous or habitual action. Vaughan (p. 134) says, "The imagery may be that of a child on a parent's lap."

In Romans 1–2 Paul gives a horrible picture of the pagan world of his day. This is corroborated by such writers as Horace, Seneca, Juvenal, and Tacitus (Robertson, p. 245). Using this figure, the pagan world had climbed up into Satan's lap and gone to sleep—the sleep of death. The alarming thing to us is that Paul's words read like a description of ungodly society today. Like its first century counterpart, our pagan social order lies in Satan's lap in a sense of false security, yet also like it, it is a seething mass of discontent. Our society seeks *life,* but in the wrong place, and all involved in it are marked by death.

On the other hand, John says, "We know [*oidamen*] that we are of God," or literally, "out of God we are." "Out of [*ek*]" refers to *source,* of which ours is God. Just as God is the extreme opposite of Satan, so is our newness of life the utter extreme from the *live-it-up-death* of which Satan is the source (see Rom. 6:23).

So resting in the assurance that we permanently have

salvation through God in Christ, we can/should yield ourselves to the Holy Spirit. Our witness in deed and word can then lead others to come out of death into life, which is possible only through regeneration, not reformation.

## V. The Christian's Relation to God (5:20)

This verse states the summit of Christian certainty. Indeed, it summarizes the message of the entire epistle. Here we have another use of *oida:* "We know with a soul-conviction which allows no debate." As previously noted, it is experiential knowledge which has been perceived to the point of absolute conviction.

What do we know? First, "that the Son of God is come." "Is come" is a present tense which carries the perfective sense: He "has come and is still here!" In John 8:42 Jesus said, literally, "For I came from God, and I am here," or "Here I am." The same verb is used in 1 John 5:20 for "is come."

Thus John reminds us of the abiding presence of Christ. This is in keeping with Jesus' promise in Matthew 28:20: "Lo, I am with you alway, even unto the end of the world." "Alway" translates "all the days"—good days and bad days; days of joy and days of sorrow; days of victory and days of defeat. It will be so "until the final consummation of the age [*sunteleia*]."

Second, we know that through Christ's coming and presence that God "hath given us an understanding, that we may know him that is true, and we are in him that is true, even in his Son Jesus Christ."

"Hath given" is a perfect tense of completeness, which

means fully given and still a present possession. What God gives is an "understanding." The Greek word means "through mind" (*dia*, through, and *noia*, referring to the mind). When our minds think through a matter we understand it.

The result of this understanding is "that [*hina*, in order that] we may know [experientially] the true one," God. Being in "the true one" refers to a vital union with God. "Even" is not in the Greek text, so a more literal reading would be, "we are in the true one in his Son Jesus Christ." Because we are united with the Father through union with the Son, the equality of the Father and Son is implied, thus declaring the full deity of Jesus Christ. So fellowship with the Father and with the Son is "one and inseparable" (Conner, p. 196).

Third, in our understanding we know that "this is the true God, and eternal life." Does "true" refer to God or to Jesus Christ? Both views have their champions. Vaughan (p. 135) notes that "his Son Jesus Christ" is "the nearer and more obvious antecedent." For this reason the idea that Jesus Christ is "the true God" should not be discounted, even though Vaughan leans toward *God*.

However, do we have to choose between the two? John has just equated Father and Son. So may we not see both persons of the Godhead as "the true God, and eternal life." "He that hath the Son hath life" (5:12a). Thus Jesus Christ is one with the Father (see John 10:30). It is through His revelation as the Son that the Father imparts eternal life.

With this John gives a final blow to the Gnostics who denied the oneness of God and Jesus Christ. Furthermore, he shows that we receive eternal life, not through the *gnōsis* of Gnosticism, but through faith in God in His person as Son.

## VI. The Closing Exhortation (5:21)

It is fitting that the apostle would close with a parting exhortation: "Little children, keep yourselves from idols." "Keep" renders *phulassō*, "to guard." According to the *Theological Dictionary of the New Testament (op cit.)*, this verb was used interchangeably with *tēreō* (see 5:18), "to stand guard." It appears only here in the epistle, and is found three times in the Gospel of John (12:25,47; 17:12). But *tēreō* appears more often: eight times in the epistle, and eighteen times in the gospel. We may see a common meaning here, since both verbs carry the idea of guarding. As Jesus Christ stands guard over His people to see that Satan does not capture them (5:18), so we are to guard ourselves "from" (*apo,* away from) idols or any substitute for God which seeks to draw us away from Him and His truth.

In this context "idols" should not be limited to graven images. An idol is anything or anyone standing between you and God. *The Amplified New Testament*'s rendering, with bracketed comments, is helpful at this point. "Little children, keep yourselves from idols—false gods, [from anything and everything that would occupy the place in your heart due to God, from any form or substitute for Him that would take first place in your life]."

John's readers were little islands of Christian truth in an ocean of paganism, whose idols were reefs upon which the unwary might crash. They were *materialism* in metal, stone, and wood. Our social order is too sophisticated to bow before such, but a materialistic age worships them in other ways.

In this context, however, it seems that the idols John has in mind are more intellectual and spiritual. This then is his final warning in the epistle against the Gnostics and their system. Throughout the letter the apostle has contrasted the false system of the Gnostic heretics with the true revelation of God in Christ. Plummer (p. 144) says an idol is whatever "usurps the place of God in the heart, whether this be a person, or a system, or a project, or wealth, or what not." So John exhorts constant vigilance against any false system or philosophy which downgrades God and His redemptive work, the eternal Christ who became flesh as Jesus of Nazareth.

In Colossians Paul is combatting the same Gnostic heresy. In 2:8-9 he wrote, "Beware lest any man spoil [take away as booty] you through philosophy and, [even] vain deceit, after the tradition of men, after the rudiments [basic elements] of the world [*kosmos*, cosmos], and not after Christ. For in him dwelleth all the fulness of the Godhead bodily." Literally verse 9 reads, "Because in him and in no one else is permanently at home every single part of the essence of deity, the state of being God in bodily form."

In Colossians we find the only use in the New Testament of the word "philosophy" (*philosophia*). ("Philosophers" [*philosophoi*] is used one time in Acts 17:18). Paul is not opposing philosophy as such, but, as the definite article with "philosophy" in Colossians 2:8 shows, a particular philosophy, namely, the Gnostic philosophy. Just as Paul warns against a philosophy characterized as empty deceit, so does John.

The late Robert G. Lee was fond of referring to false teachings as "isms" that should be "wasms." This is in complete agreement with John's message in his first epistle. Thus it was for his time and for all time.

# 2 JOHN

# TEN
## To The
## "Elect Lady"

*2 John 1-13*

---

### Outline

I. The Salutation (vv. 1-3)
II. The Occasion of the Letter (v. 4)
III. The Exhortations and Warnings (vv. 5-11)
    1. The exhortation to love and obedience
       (vv. 5-6)
    2. The warning against false doctrine
       (vv. 7-9)
    3. The warning against aiding false
       teachers (vv. 10-11)
IV. The Conclusion (vv. 12-13)

---

Several years ago Billy Graham came to Oklahoma City to speak at a citywide religious rally. Prior to his arrival a lady called me about her mother who was confined to her bed in a small nursing home. Her only touch with religious services was by radio and television. Although she was not a Baptist, Billy was her favorite preacher, and she thought of him as her pastor.

Knowing that he would be in the city only a few hours, the daughter said what a blessing it would be to her mother if he would see her, but the daughter would understand if he could not go. She would not tell her mother lest she be disappointed.

When he arrived at the airport I told him about the mother, but assured him he did not have to go. He said, "Of course we will go!"

At the nursing home he walked into her room where she was propped up in bed. He said, "I am Billy Graham." Seeing that she did not believe it, he repeated, "I really am Billy Graham, and I have come to see you!" Suddenly, as it dawned upon her that it was he, her mouth dropped open and her eyes were opened wide. Then in excitement she started talking, so that he could hardly stop her. Finally he said, "Well I must go. But let us pray together."

As we drove away I thought, "Here is a man who has the ear of kings, queens, and the other leaders of the nations of the world. In his worldwide ministry he has preached to more people than any other man who ever lived. Yet he had time to minister to one little bedfast lady in a small nursing home." More than audiences with world leaders and preaching to countless throngs, this incident showed the stature of the man and the bigness of his spirit.

In this we see a replica of the character of the apostle John. Though he understood and interpreted the person and work of Jesus more intimately than any other writer in the New Testament, and though he was in a life and death struggle with evil, he took time to pen this little personal note to one Christian woman, bringing joy to her heart and strengthening her in her own battle with evil forces which swirled about her. In this letter written on a single piece of "paper" (v. 12), he has blessed uncounted souls through the centuries.

To the "Elect Lady"

## I. The Salutation (vv. 1-3)

Second John begins with a salutation which contains many of the standard features used in correspondence of that age. Yet it also contains a very personal tone, as would be expected between two friends. However, McDowell (p. 225) points out that the letter itself is more formal than thousands of other papyrus letters which have been found. This is understandable in light of its contents and purpose. (See the later discussion as to the identity of "the elect lady.")

The author calls himself simply "the elder" (*ho presbuteros*, note, "Presbyterian" v. 1). The identity of this "elder" is a matter of dispute. Eusebius (*Eccles. Hist.*, 3.39) quotes Papias (early second century A.D.) as referring to the apostles as elders. But Papias also speaks of an Elder John, said to be living at that time and from whom Papias learned much about the apostles and their teachings. From this brief reference comes the contention that this obscure Elder John wrote the Johannine epistles as well as the Fourth Gospel. But Robertson (p. 249) notes that as early as 1911 Dom Chapman in *John the Presbyter and the Fourth Gospel* disproved his existence. However, this vaporous figure still exists in the minds of many.

The New Testament supports Papias' statement about apostles being called elders (see 1 Pet. 5:1). The style of the Fourth Gospel and these three epistles strongly supports the argument that they had a common authorship. Even though this author does not name himself, evidence strongly suggests that he was the apostle John. We assume that he was the author of these writings, plus Revelation, where for the purpose of authenticating that work he does use his name (1:9).

"Elder" could mean "old man", or be an official title, with the latter being more likely. Among the Jews the word originally denoted an old man, who by virtue of age was capable of giving wise counsel. In the Sanhedrin "elder" was used as a title (see Matt. 16:21). It also was used among Christians to denote pastors of churches (Acts 20:17), which is evidently how it is used here.

The term "elect lady" also poses a problem. Many modern interpreters identify her as a church (McDowell, p. 226). However, a more convincing argument can be made for the reference to a Christian woman. *The Twentieth Century New Testament* renders it "an eminent Christian lady." It has even been suggested that either of the words "elect" *(eklektos)* or "lady" *(kuria)* could be the recipient's personal name, either *Eklecta* or *Cyria.* But probably it means simply "elect lady", or as the *New English Bible* reads, "a Lady chosen by God."

The address also includes "her children." "Whom" is a masculine pronoun, including both the lady and her children. "I" is emphatic, being written out as well as present in the verb "love" *(agapaō),* the verb for Christian love. In the Greek text "truth" is without the definite article, so "in sincerity" is a better translation. Weymouth renders it "truly love." With the definite article it denotes the truth of the gospel, or since Jesus Christ is "the truth" (John 14:6), it could mean those who *know* the Lord Jesus as Savior. Jesus, the true revelation of God in His saving purpose, abides in us, and will do so "for ever" or "unto [throughout] the age" (v. 2).

Verse 3 is not a prayer but a statement of assurance, as seen in the future tense "be" ("shall be"). He is confident that grace, mercy, and peace from God the Father and Jesus Christ His Son will be with them in truth and love.

## II. The Occasion of the Letter (v. 4).

The epistle does not reveal the residence of the addressee, but most likely it was somewhere in the Roman province of Asia, probably Ephesus. Perhaps she lived in another city than the one in which John lived. In either case, he had come into contact with her children.

The Greek text reads "out of [*ek*] your children." Robertson (p. 27) reads "certain of thy children," which suggests that she had other children also. Therefore John had found some of them "walking in truth" (no definite article in the Greek text). "Truth" renders the same word in verse 1a which carries the idea of sincerity. They were sincerely ordering their conduct in keeping with "a commandment" which Christians had received from the Father. John does not specify the commandment, but probably he had 1 John 3:23 in mind: "And this is his commandment, That ye should believe on the name of his Son Jesus Christ, and love one another, as he gave us commandment" (see John 15:12). Their faith in Jesus Christ had not been corrupted by the Gnostics, and they were keeping His commandment to love one another as He loved them.

So John wrote this joyful letter to his friend the "elect lady." With a mother's love and prayer she had followed her children who were away from home. Certainly to receive this brief note from John comforted and thrilled her heart.

Since retiring from the pastorate I have handled my correspondence by hand. At first I felt apologetic about subjecting people to trying to decipher my "hen-scratching." But to my delight I have discovered two things. Since I do my own writing, I can say more with fewer words than when my secretary typed my dictation. And people appreciate a handwritten letter more than one that is typed.

What a treasure it would be to have a brief, personal note written by the apostle John! And what a blessing it has been to millions of people, that this "elect lady" preserved hers so that under the guidance of the Holy Spirit it was included in the Bible!

## III. The Exhortations and Warnings (vv. 5-11)

John also used this commendatory note to exhort the mother to emulate her children's conduct. He also warned against those whose teachings were designed to lead her astray.

### 1. The exhortation to love and obedience (vv. 5-6)

"Beseech" renders a verb meaning "to pray," which means he was not praying to her, but pleading with her. John may have used this word to express the earnestness of his request. Concerning the reference to a "new commandment" see 1 John 2:7-8.

This is not a new commandment, but an old one which the Lord gave to His people: "that we love one another" (v. 5). He calls upon the "lady" *(kuria)* that she continue to live a life of Christian love *(agapaō)*. This was/is all the more necessary in light of the *hatred* Christians receive from an unregenerated social order. Bound together in such love enables the Lord's people to resist persecution, whether physical, mental, or spiritual.

In verse 6 John further defines this love. The text reads literally, "And this is the love." Note the definite article which points to a particular kind of love. Unfortunately, the English language has only one word for "love" as such, and even that one word in recent years has been degraded in popular usage. But the Greek language had three words that expressed different kinds of love (see p. 107). In the New Testament *agapē* expresses a love which characterizes the nature of God (1 John 4:16). It is the love we should have for God, and is the love which in Christ believers have for one another (see 1 Cor. 13, "charity," KJV, which translates this word). As stated in our treatment of 1 John, W. Hersey Davis once said that the English word which most nearly translates *agapē* is "selflessness." "Selfishness" is the root of all sin; "selflessness" is the source of this "God-kind-of-love."

"The commandment" singles out one particular commandment, that we love one another. "Walk" is used often in the New Testament for one's manner of life. Thus our life-style is to be characterized by selfless love. It is rooted in God, and expresses itself toward both God and man. It is "to live in the spirit of love" (TCNT).

2. The warning against false doctrine (vv. 7-9)

The need for Christians loving one another is accented by the fact that "many deceivers are entered into the world" (v. 7), and they are still with us! "Deceivers" renders *planoi* (note "planet"). The ancients thought of the planets as wandering bodies, so the idea in "deceivers" is those who wish to lead believers astray. This is a reference to both Cerinthian and Docetic Gnostics, since both groups denied "that Jesus Christ is come in the flesh."

Note the combination "Jesus Christ." As noted previously (see Introduction, "III. Purpose"), the Cerinthian Gnostics, who denied the deity of Jesus, taught that

Christ was neither born nor did He die, that He came upon the man Jesus at His baptism and left Him on the cross. The Docetic Gnostics, who denied the humanity of Christ, said that He did not have a flesh and blood body but only *seemed* (*dokeō*, I seem) to have fleshly existence.

These are "the deceiver and the antichrist," both of which in the Greek text have the definite article. Goodspeed reads, "That is the mark of the imposter and the Antichrist." The *New English Bible* says, "These are the persons described as the Antichrist, the arch-deceiver." John is not necessarily thinking eschatologically, but was dealing with a situation in existence in Asia during the latter half of the first century and beyond—even today. Anyone who denies the full deity-humanity of Jesus Christ today is a neo-Gnostic.

Because of these false teachers John warns the "elect lady" and her children, indeed all believers, to "look to yourselves." "Look" (from *blepō*) is a present imperative form, and could be interpreted, therefore, as a command for constant watchfulness. But in this context it more likely expresses urgency, perhaps like our "Look out!" The reflexive pronoun means that each Christian must be on guard with respect to himself.

The best Greek texts of verse 8b read "you," not "we." "That ye lose not those things which we have wrought." John warns against the danger of losing their Christian faith in which he and others had established them. "Don't throw away all the labor that has been spent on you" (Phillips). Again, the best texts of verse 8c read "you" instead of "we." "But a full reward ye may receive." The "full reward" does not involve regeneration but glorification for the faithful. Degrees of reward in heaven will be determined by the believer's faithfulness in the state of sanctification. John wants the best for his Christian friends.

In verse 9 "transgresseth" should read "whosoever goeth onward." The verb *proagō* literally means "to go on before" (see Mark 11:9). Here "goeth onward" is the same as "and abideth not in the doctrine [teaching] of Christ." It is not teachings about Christ, but what He taught. The reference is to the Gnostic teachers who claimed that their system of thought went beyond God's revelation in Christ. Claiming to be advanced thinkers, they wanted "to relegate Christ to the past in their onward march" (Robertson, p. 254). Robertson rightly raises the question: "Is he a 'landmark' merely or is he our goal and pattern? Progress we all desire, but progress toward Christ, not away from him . . . Jesus Christ is still ahead of us all calling us to come on to him."

The intensity of John's feelings about this is seen in his words about such false teachers: "God they do not have." Abiding in the teaching of Christ is evidence that one is a Christian. Such keeps on having both the Father and the Son. Jesus regarded Himself and His Father as inseparable, despite what some so-called progressive thinkers might say.

These statements emphasize John's feelings about the Gnostics not having God, and also stress his admonition to be faithful to the teaching of Christ which they had received.

These words of John were timely and are timeless. We should beware of anyone who claims to have any new revelation from God which is contrary to His revelation in Jesus Christ. Revelation and inspiration as the Bible presents them have ended with the New Testament. Beyond that we have illumination by the Holy Spirit to enable us to understand the revelation already given. As John says in 1 John 4:1-2, we must be certain that one speaks by the Holy Spirit and not by the evil spirit. The latter produces false prophets and teachers.

No matter how cleverly one may speak, we should be as the Bereans. When Paul came preaching that Jesus was the Christ of the Old Testament, "they received the word with all readiness of mind, and searched the scriptures daily, whether those things were so" (Acts 17:11). They listened with open minds, but they checked this new message against the teachings of their Scriptures (Old Testament). Finding that he had spoken the truth, they believed. Had it not been the truth they would have rejected it. In no uncertain terms Paul taught that Christians should continue to do so (see Gal. 1:6-9). If we do the same, "isms" would soon be "wasms."

3. The warning against aiding false teachers (vv. 10-11)

The Gnostics, as well as many other false teachers, went from place to place peddling their vicious wares. Thus John warned against giving aid to such: "If there come any unto you, and bring not this doctrine, receive him not into your house, neither bid him God speed" (v. 10). This is an obvious reference to false teachers, specifically the Gnostics.

The New Testament urges Christians to show hospitality to strangers (see 1 Tim. 5:10; Heb. 13:2). In fact "hospitality" translates a word which means love of strangers. Public lodging facilities were bad at the best, and there were few fit places for Christians to stay, morally or otherwise. Most of the New Testament references concerning hospitality refer to Christians who were passing through, especially missionaries.

But John has quite a different situation in mind. He is

thinking of false teachers whom he has called "antichrist" which means just that—anti-Christ. Christians are not to welcome them into their homes, or to bid them "God speed," or to wish them well when they leave. This shows how serious this Gnostic problem was. For one thing the host family could be contaminated by these false teachings. Furthermore, these teachers could use their hospitality, by *name-dropping*, to gain entrance to another Christian's home along the way, starting a vicious cycle. At that time churches met in homes (see Rom. 16:5; Col. 4:15; Philemon 2c), so not only homes but churches could be wrecked as well.

"Receive him not into your house" may also read "not to be at home to such." The supposition here is regarding those known to be false teachers. If Abraham "entertained angels unawares" (Heb. 13:2), indiscriminate hospitality could also mean that we entertain devils unawares, or with full awareness if the host knows them for what they are. In so doing, the one guilty of such becomes "partaker of his evil deeds" (v. 11). "Is partaker" translates the verb which means "to share." This use of "to share" is apparently the same as it is often used in the papyri. Even though you may not agree with his teachings, you aid and abet him in his evil work, thus you share in it. As Robertson (p. 255) says, "There was [is] no way of escaping responsibility for the harm wrought by these propagandists of evil. It is not a case of mere hospitality to strangers."

## IV. The Conclusion (vv. 12-13)

The epistle closes on a personal note. John still had many things he wished to write to his friend, but he would not do so "with paper and ink" (v. 12). "Paper" (*chartēs*) was made out of the papyrus plant which grew along the Nile River in Egypt. One may still see small portions of it there. This *paper* was made out of the pith of the plant. Strips of it were laid in layers on top of each other at right angles, were wetted down, and then pressed together. Basically the process was something like making paper out of wood pulp today. The sheets were dried in the sun and then smoothed by using a bone or piece of shell. The sheets were about five by nine or eleven inches in size. They were glued together into rolls for use in writing lengthy documents.

John probably used one small sheet for writing this letter. Vaughan (p. 13) suggests that one reason for not writing more was that he had used up his papyrus. The "ink" was made of soot or lampblack, water, and gum.

John trusts (hopes, *elpizō*) to see the "elect lady" soon, and to talk with her "face to face" (literally, mouth to mouth, *stoma pros stoma*). Probably he would tell her more good things about her children, which would gladden any mother's heart. Some manuscripts read "your" (*humōn*), while others read "our" (*hēmōn*); probably "our" is correct. Such a personal visit would completely fulfill (perfect tense) their joy.

John's final word is a greeting from "the children of thy elect sister" (v. 13). This evidently was another Christian lady, sister of the lady to whom John wrote.

Thus closes this delightfully personal but extremely practical note from the aged apostle, which probably was written by his own hand. It shines as a small but bright star in the galaxy of the New Testament.

# 3 JOHN

# ELEVEN

# The Profile Of
# Early Church Life

## 3 John 1-14

---

### Outline

I. The Greeting (v. 1)
II. The Prayer and Commendation of Gaius (vv. 2-8)
III. The Condemnation of Diotrephes (vv. 9-11)
IV. The Commendation of Demetrius (v. 12)
V. The Conclusion (vv. 13-14)

---

Some years ago someone wrote a fictional book about a church, its life and its people. As I read it, I laughed heartily and recalled similar people and events in my own ministry which were no laughing matter at the time. Someone else who had read it asked me if there were such a church. I replied, "Yes, honey, there is. Once I was its pastor!"

Of course, I spoke in jest. Yet at the same time it was a cross-section of church life. It presented the good and faithful as well as the problem people. My old teacher, A. T. Robertson, was fond of telling us that when we were in the pastorate we must love the people, "warts and all." Every church has both.

It is against such a background that we can best understand 3 John. For its message centers about three people:

Gaius, Diotrephes, and Demetrius. John's first two epistles deal with the problem of the Gnostics, who as outsiders sought to ravish the faithful. His third epistle gives us a brief glance inside one of the churches, depicting both the good and bad sides. Thus John enables us to look into this *mirror* in order to examine ourselves and our churches today. Because of its nature 3 John is personal in tone.

## I. The Greeting (v. 1)

"The elder unto the wellbeloved Gaius, whom I love in truth." "The elder" is the same as the author of 2 John. Twice in this brief verse he expresses his love for his dear friend "Gaius." Four times John calls him "beloved" (vv. 1,2,5,11; see 2 John 1 for the same phrase "whom I love in truth" or love sincerely). Goodspeed reads, "to my dear friend Gaius;" Weymouth has "whom I truly love."

Gaius is not identified further. However, three friends of Paul are mentioned by this name: Gaius of Macedonia (Acts 19:29); Gaius of Derbe (Acts 20:4), and Gaius of Corinth (1 Cor. 1:14). It was one of the most common names in the Roman empire. Probably this is yet another Gaius who was John's friend.

We have no idea of what church Gaius was a part, but in 3 John 9 there is a possible reference to 2 John. If this is true, then Gaius and the "elect lady" were in the same church—a loyal and beloved man and woman.

## II. The Prayer for and Commendation of Gaius (vv. 2-8)

Through the years when I have signed an autograph I

write under my name "III John 2." It is John's prayer for his beloved friend. The word "wish" (KJV) renders a word for praying *(euchomai)*. "Above" translates *peri*, which means "concerning," or "around." The text may read, "In all things I pray" or "continue to pray." Whatever else John might include in his prayers for Gaius, he always prayed for his wellbeing. "Prospereth" *(euodoō, eu,* well, *hodos,* way) means to have a prosperous journey; John also prays for his health.

But he adds one thing: "even as thy soul prospereth", or "keeps on prospering." "Soul" *(psuchē)* in this context means the principle of higher life or the spiritual part of his being. He prays that, as he prospers spiritually, he will also prosper materially and physically. Therefore, John prays that Gaius will live a balanced life: a healthy soul in a healthy body, enjoying all the good things God gives him; a good journey indeed!

From praying, John turns to commendation. He tells of his great joy when his friends "repeatedly came" and "repeatedly bore witness" (present tenses) of "the truth that is in thee" (v. 3). In the Greek text the possessive pronoun precedes the noun, emphasizing "your." So the translation could be, "of your truth", or "your sincerity of life." "Even as thou walkest in the truth". "Truth" without the definite article means that he ordered his life in sincerity, and that he was true to Christ. This could be a veiled reference to Gaius' faithful life, despite Gnostic temptations to live otherwise.

John has no greater joy than to hear that his "children" are walking in "the truth" (v. 4). Here the definite article points to the truth that is in Christ. Note the apostle's emphasis upon truth in the first four verses. "Children" suggests that Gaius may have been one of John's converts.

In any case, it was John's favorite term for those to whom he ministered (see 1 John).

John next commends Gaius for his hospitality "to the brethren, and [even] to strangers" (vv. 5-8). The particle *kai* may read "and", or "even." The latter seems to fit better here. This is reflected in the *New English Bible:* "for these our fellow-Christians, strangers though they are to you." Alford's *The New Testament* reads "to the brethren, who besides are strangers." We noted in 2 John the emphasis the early Christians placed upon opening their homes to fellow-believers who travelled.

Gaius' hospitality had been reported openly to "the church," probably the one in Ephesus (v. 6). "Bring forward on their journey" means more than saying "God bless you" as they leave. Dating back to the time of Homer (*Od.* XV. 74), it was customary "to speed the parting guest, and sometimes accompanying him, sometimes providing money and food. Rabbis were so escorted and Paul alludes to the same custom in Rom. 15:24 and Titus 3:13" (Robertson, p. 261).

"After a godly sort" (*axiōs tou Theou*) means "worthily of God." Holtzmann (quoted by Robertson) says, "Since they are God's representatives, treat them as you would God" (see John 13:20).

That Gaius provided them with food and money is evident in verse 7. Since his guests went forth "for [*huper*, on behalf of] his [Christ's] name's sake," they were travelling missionaries. Because of his generous help in lodging, food, and money they did not need to take anything (nothing receiving) from (*apo*) the Gentiles or pagans. Many teachers went about teaching for money, but had these Christians done so, they would have been classed as mercenaries rather than missionaries. In 1 Corinthians 9

Paul insisted that preachers were worthy of monetary support from those to whom they ministered. Despite this principle, he took nothing from the Corinthians, because the Judaizers accused him of preaching for money. In our day missionaries give their lives, but they should be supported by other Christians and not be dependent upon those among whom they serve.

John states the principle in verse 8 that we are under obligation to receive or help missionaries. "That" introduces a purpose clause: "In order that we may keep on becoming fellow-workers with" or "for the truth," that is, the truth of the gospel. The alternate reading may mean that we are co-workers with the missionaries for the truth, or it can mean co-workers with the truth. In any case, by sharing with those who preach the gospel, we are partners in the missionary enterprise. In your body you may not be called or able to go throughout the world preaching the gospel, but you can do so with your gifts. Thus you become a *missionary*, and share the responsibility with those called to give their lives in this blessed vocation.

Although we need more missionaries and evangelists, we also need more people like Gaius who refresh those who are sent by God. One mission board reports that it has more mission volunteers than it has funds. God is calling each of us to be a Gaius through whom this situation may be rectified.

## III. The Condemnation of Diotrephes (vv. 9-11)

The opposite of Gaius is Diotrephes. "I wrote unto the church" (v. 9). What John wrote is a matter of speculation. Is this a reference to 2 John? It could be, if one sees the "elect lady" (2 John 1) as a church. However, we have noted that it probably refers to a noble Christian lady. Was it a lost letter, as some suppose? This suggests a letter of no importance to the Holy Spirit, or else it would have been preserved for the canon of Scripture. But coming from an apostle, no letter would be unimportant. Was it simply a brief note of introduction from John to the church regarding certain people, such as travelling missionaries? This concern fits the context better than any other.

Whatever it was that John wrote, he says that "Diotrephes . . . receiveth us not," which means that he refused to accept John's note or word. He rejected the apostle's authority by refusing to permit the ones sent by John to preach in the church. If John ever planned to visit the church again, he apparently expected a hostile reception, based on Diotrephes' past behavior (v. 10).

Who was Diotrephes? He appears nowhere else in the New Testament. He is described as one "who loveth to have the preeminence among them," or in the church. "Loveth to have the preeminence" translates one word (*philoprōteuō*), which means, "to desire first place." He may have been the pastor of the church, but since the pastor would be more likely to respect John's apostolic authority, he probably was some other church leader, maybe a deacon. McDowell (p. 230) suggests that he may have been the church moderator, or chairman of the deacons. Whoever he was, he desired to rule the entire church. Years ago I declined to be called to a church. I did not feel led to accept it. One of the main reasons was that about every matter I discussed with the pulpit committee, they said they would need to confer with a certain member about it.

A. T. Robertson (p. 263) tells about writing an article

on Diotrephes for a denominational paper. After it was published, the editor told him of receiving letters from twenty-five deacons who cancelled their subscriptions to protest against being publicly attacked in the paper.

But whether Diotrephes was a pastor or deacon, there is no place for a *boss* in a New Testament church! Both pastor and deacon are but servants, with the earthly authority residing in the local congregation. Of course, the ultimate authority is Christ. A local New Testament church is one which operates through democratic processes under the Lordship of Jesus Christ.

"Wherefore" (v. 10) refers back to verse 9. "If I come" means that he hopes to visit this church in person. In the event that he does make this visit, he will "remember" or "bring to remembrance" the things which Diotrephes keeps on doing. This is a threat to defy Diotrephes and to expose him publicly before the church. The aged apostle is not afraid of this self-appointed tyrant. John is the apostle of love, but despite his age he is still a *son of thunder* (Mark 3:17) when the occasion calls for it.

The apostle proceeds to describe the actions of Diotrephes (v. 10): "Prating against us with malicious words." In the Greek text "with malicious [wicked] words" comes first, so they are emphatic. "Prating", to accuse idly or falsely, is a present participle, that is, he keeps on doing this. He would not receive, or show hospitality to, the brethren whom John had sent, nor would he permit others to do so. Instead he cast them out of the church. "Them" evidently refers to the ones who wanted to receive John's brethren. It has been suggested that Diotrephes may have been a wealthy slave owner whose slaves were the Christians he cast out. However, his attitude was such that it might apply to anyone. "Casteth out" renders the word

*ekballō,* which was used in John 2:15 of Jesus driving from
the temple those who profaned it with their wares. Also it
was used in John 9:34-35 of the Jewish leaders casting out
the healed blind man. Perhaps this could mean excom-
munication, but probably it means simply evicting them
bodily.

John urges his friends not to follow, imitate *(mimeomai)*
or copy such evil action, but to follow the good (v. 11).
This is probably a contrast between Diotrephes and Demetrius whom he introduces in verse 12. "He that doeth
good is of [*ek,* out of] God [a Christian]: but he that doeth
evil hath not seen God" at any time, much less experienced him. Knox reads "the wrong-doer has caught no
glimpse of him."

From the Greek text "doeth good" *(agathopoieō)* and
"doeth evil" *(kakopoieō)* mean "to have the habit of" or
practicing such. That outer conduct reveals one's inner
condition is John's principle by which he judges that
Diotrephes was not even a Christian. If he had been, he
would have acted differently. Strong condemnation, but
true.

## IV. The Commendation of Demetrius (v. 12)

Demetrius stands out in contrast to Diotrephes. No one
spoke any good of the latter, but everyone bears witness as
to the genuine Christian character of Demetrius. His life
squares with the truth itself, that of the gospel.

Concerning Demetrius' Christian character, John adds
his own testimony, which his readers know is true. "We
. . . our" are literary plurals, referring to John. Nothing
else is known about Demetrius. It is also the name of the

silversmith who started the riot against Paul (Acts 19:24,38). Some have suggested that he later became a Christian, and is the Demetrius mentioned here. We can hope so, but there is no record of it. These are the only two occurrences of Demetrius in the New Testament. Even if they are not the same person, it is interesting that they both lived in Ephesus. In any case, John's Demetrius was most likely the bearer of this letter, and could have carried the one to the "elect lady" also.

## V. The Conclusion (vv. 13-14)

As in 2 John, here John says that he "had many things to write" (v. 13). "Had" is an imperfect tense. He had many things in mind when he started writing, "But I do not will with ink and pen to write." The pen was a reed used for writing on papyrus and parchment.

Instead of writing, he hopes to see them soon (v. 14). Then he will speak to them "face to face" (see 2 John 12). The apostle closes by wishing that they may have peace (They needed it with Diotrephes around!) and by sending greetings from those in Ephesus. As was the custom in papyri letters, he asks that they be greeted by name since he knew them all. But with John it was not mere form, but an expression of genuine love.

# Bibliography

Barclay, William. *The Letters of John and Jude.* Philadelphia: The Westminster Press, 1958.

Blailock, E. M. *Faith Is the Victory: Studies in the First Epistle of John.* Grand Rapids: William B. Eerdmans, 1959.

Brooke, A. E. *A Critical and Exegetical Commentary on the Johannine Epistles.* The International Critical Commentary, vol. 43. Edinburgh: T. and T. Clark, 1912.

Calvin, John. *Commentaries on the Catholic Epistles.* Grand Rapids: William B. Eerdmans, 1959.

Conner. W. T. *The Epistles of John: Their Meaning and Message.* New York: Fleming H. Revell Co., 1929.

Law, Robert. *The Tests of Life: A Study of the First Epistle of John.* Edinburgh: T. and T. Clark, 1909.

McDowell, Edward A. *1-2-3 John.* Broadman Bible Commentary, vol. 12. Nashville: Broadman Press, 1972.

McNeile, A. H. *An Introduction to the Study of the New Testament.* 2nd ed., revised by C. S. C. Williams. Oxford: The Clarendon Press, 1953.

Plummer, Alfred. *The Epistles of St. John.* Cambridge Greek Testament, vols. 23-24. Cambridge: Cambridge Press, 1938.

Ramsay, Alexander. *The Revelation and the Johannine Epistles.* The Westminster New Testament. New York: Fleming H. Revell Co., n. d.

Robertson, A. T. *Word Pictures in the New Testament,* vol. 6. Nashville: Broadman Press, 1933.

Ross, Alexander. *The Epistles of James and John.* The New International Commentary on the New Testament. Grand Rapids: William B. Eerdmans, 1954.

Smith, David. *The Epistles of John.* The Expositor's Greek Testament, vol. 5. Grand Rapids: William B. Eerdmans, 1951.

Vaughan, Curtis. *1, 2, 3 John: A Study Guide.* Grand Rapids: Zondervan Publishing House, 1970.

Westcott, Brooke Foss. *The Epistles of St. John.* Cambridge: Macmillan and Company, 1892.